THE 7 STEPS TO IGNITE
FLOURISHING IN LEADERS, TEAMS AND ORGANIZATIONS
POSITIVITY PULSE ACTION GUIDE

Alletta Bayer, MA
Sherry Blair

This Action Guide is a quick start
implementation guide and coaching support for
The Positivity Pulse: Transforming Your Workplace
by Sherry Blair with Melissa Lynn Block

Visit **SherryBlairInstitute.com** for additional
information, free downloads, and resources.

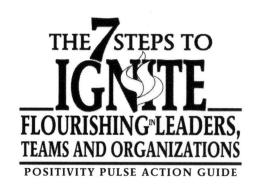

THE 7 STEPS TO
IGNITE
FLOURISHING IN LEADERS,
TEAMS AND ORGANIZATIONS
POSITIVITY PULSE ACTION GUIDE

SherryBlairInstitute.com

Character Illustrations by: Brenda Brown
www.webtoon.com

Cover Design, Graphics, and Page Layout by: Kristine Requena
KristineRequena.MyPortfolio.com

ISBN-10: 1489571159
ISBN-13: 978-1489571151

Table of Contents

Worksheet List

Dear Fellow Leader,

Maybe you are looking for just a little more positive energy and good will in your relationships at work. Perhaps you feel you are "almost there" and with just a little more "something" you would flourish. Or maybe you feel so much negativity that you can hardly stand to go to work each day, but you would really like to discover how to turn that around. If so, these 7 Steps are for you.

Whether you are in need of some personal help, or your whole team or organization is on a mission to raise its level of positive energy and happiness, you can learn ways to achieve your goal doing what countless others have done. These steps will teach you how, and doing the exercises will empower you to be the change you want to experience.

As you work with intention through the steps and incorporate your new skills into your daily life, you will be amazed as you observe the changing quality of your relationships. If your whole team is committed and practicing, you may even sense a new "lightness," or what we call a *Positivity Pulse*, in your workplace.

We designed this program to take you through a 7 Step process. There might be times during this program when you may find yourself wanting to skip a step or change things around. If you come up against these desires, that's when it's important to stick with the process because often times the areas in which we want to spend the least amount of time and energy are exactly the areas where we need more understanding or are the weakest and need the most practice. By focusing in on the 7 Steps you will learn about and practicing the exercises, you'll experience incredible results.

Working through each step in order builds a strong foundation for positive change and personal transformation. Each week as you learn and practice new skills you will be building an upward spiral of positivity, leading to an expansive, flourishing life. As so often in life, the more you practice, the better you get.

And that's what this program is ultimately about: POSITIVE RESULTS.

Commit!

Practice!

Transform and Flourish!

To your success,

Alletta & Sherry

Guide to Success

Here are some suggestions for working the steps of your Action Guide.

1. This program is designed in 7 Steps. Working through each step in order will open your eyes to the important role positivity plays in transforming your life from ordinary to flourishing.

2. Have a copy of *The Positivity Pulse: Transforming Your Workplace* by Sherry Blair with Melissa Lynn Block handy for quick referral. You will need it especially for Module 1, and it will enrich your experience and understanding if you read the corresponding chapter recommended at the beginning of each Module. To access the Creative Recognitions, Inc. story, go to **YouTube**, Creative Recognitions Inc., Narrative. To order copies in bulk, email us at **info@SherryBlairInstitute.com**

3. Complete each section and relentlessly practice as if your life depends upon it. Remember: *No Practice = No Change*.

4. Don't skip over the worksheets. They help you incorporate the learning.

5. Using the Journal and Worksheet pages will give you the opportunity to explore topics, find clarity, and deepen your experience. If you have the electronic version you can choose to type your answers or print out to handwrite them. You can choose to share your thoughts with your team or keep them private.

6. If you are working on the Action Guide with your team, set and attend regular in-person, phone or online meetings, and be sure to complete each section prior to your meetings.

7. If practicing the methods feels a little strange to you at first, congratulations! Feeling a little (or a lot) out of your comfort zone means you are stretching—and learning new, positive habits. Practice more!

8. Grab an accountability buddy to practice with to stretch into those new ways of being. Remember (again!): *No Practice = No Change*.

9. Use your Assessment Worksheets to track your progress.

Visit us at www.PositivityPulse.com

POSITIVITY
PULSE

Recognizing the problem most business leaders face today, the late Peter Drucker made an astute observation in alignment with our own.

"Half the leaders I've met don't need to learn what to do. They need to learn what to stop."

But stop what? And how?

The "what" to stop and the "how" is what we are all about. It is our mission to ignite flourishing qualities and experiences of leaders, teams, and organizations by teaching people *how to stop* what is not working and *how to change* it. If you study our logo, you will see a "pulse line" or heartbeat symbol. To us, this beat is symbolic of the "energy pulse" of the individuals in an organization, as well as the "pulse" of the whole organization. To illustrate this concept in the extremes, a "flat-lined" pulse indicates disengaged and failing employees better known as "dead people working" or a flat-lined organization, and a frenetic pulse indicates stressed and crazed employees. Conversely, a robustly beating steady pulse, what we call a "Positivity Pulse," indicates happy, productive, flourishing employees with high energy and engaged momentum in a positive direction.

Flat-Lined Pulse

Frenetic Pulse

Positivity Pulse

Two Secrets

Negativity lurks in many forms—all costly in many ways:

- Disgruntled employees, bad attitudes, and low morale.

- Stubbornly low or falling rates of productivity.

- Shrinking bottom line.

- Internal conflict and arguing among teams or across the company.

- Excessive sick days.

- Employees just giving their minimum efforts.

- High turnover rates.

But since negativity has an energetic quality to it, if the negativity were to stop, there would be a big energy void to fill. If this talk of energy sounds "woo-woo" to you, just stop and think for a moment. When someone is acting out in a negative way, how does that make you feel? In descriptive American slang terms, you might say they are a "downer." That is the perfect way to describe negativity in one word, because negative energy is a contagious downer. It brings everyone "down" a few notches in energy level. And it's difficult, if not impossible, to keep bringing your best efforts and creativity to a negative workplace.

Conversely, when someone expresses excitement about something in a positive way, you might say they are "upbeat." You can feel this because positive energy is also contagious, and even just one happy, excited person positively affects the energy of everyone receiving their positive communications. (Fredrickson, 2009) It has been revealed by Barbara Fredrickson, Keenan Distinguished Professor in the Department of Psychology at the University of North Carolina Chapel Hill, a guru in the study of positive emotions, that energetically we are indeed changing at the cellular level when we increase positivity. That's because positivity raises the level of the hormone oxytocin, which ignites more brainpower and gives us that "feel good" energy that also increases our overall well-being. (Fredrickson, 2013)

Increasing positive emotions at work can:

- Cut costs by enabling employees to improve efficiency.

- Increase performance and productivity.

- Transform people and help them become their best.

- Build better interpersonal skills and team collaboration.

- Reduce the cost of sick leaves.

- Reduce the cost of employee turnover.

- Build better customer relationships. (Pryce-Jones, 2010)

Now you need the second "secret" in order to get a Positivity Pulse in yourself or your organization so you hum along like a finely tuned instrument together with happy, engaged, loyal employees contributing positively toward your goals. The second secret is learning *how* to fill that energy void left from removing negative energy with the higher energy of positivity. Conscientiously working and practicing the 7 Steps of this workbook will empower you to implement the "how." It's easy when you go step-by-step.

The choice is simple and the choice is yours. You can transform to a happier and more engaged person who is flourishing. And your organization can become a happier and more positive and productive place to work. These 7 Steps will show you how. It all begins with a decision to learn and practice new habits. At this instant, you can decide.

Your partners in positivity,

Alletta & Sherry

Let's Jump Into Action!

MODULE 1

Mindset
Open to Experiencing Yourself and Others

THE 7 STEPS TO IGNITE FLOURISHING IN LEADERS, TEAMS AND ORGANIZATIONS is about discovering how to create an upward spiral of positive feelings and experiences for yourself and others in everyday activities. Living a flourishing life, a fuller, richer, happier, more expansive life—that's what it's all about.

 One of the secrets of learning how is to open your eyes to the positive inquiry of "what is strong" about a situation instead of negatively asking "what is wrong." Learning to look for what is going right in a person or situation involves sharpening your powers of observation—both of yourself and others around you. Reading the illustrative tale *Creative Recognitions* in Exercise 1 will introduce you to characters with different styles of relating. You just might recognize yourself in the mix!

Module 1 Objectives

- To open your awareness of the various positive and negative behavioral characteristics of workplace communications between yourself and others.

- To realize you have a habitual way of relating and communicating—and that you can add more positivity with conscious intention and action.

- To understand the power and impact that people's choice of thoughts, attitudes, words and tone has in workplace communications.

- To examine the current culture of your workplace and the benefits of human capital.

- To understand the importance of choosing an intention to assist you in having clarity about the outcome you want from this program.

Module 1 Summary

- Negativity and fear-based communications from leadership might work short term to get leaders what they want, but a negative environment creates big problems later, such as contentious relationships, sabotage and lower productivity, retention, and morale. Discouraged, the recipient of negativity spirals down and frequently makes even more negative behavioral choices as well as unintentional errors in their output. (Pryce-Jones, 2010)

- *Appropriate* negative emotions such as grieving, anger at being abused, fear of something that could harm us, etc., are useful and important to our well-being. In building a Positivity Pulse the goal is to reduce ***inappropriate*** or ***gratuitous*** negativity.

- All staff best develop on a positive trajectory and flourish when they are regularly "fed" with detailed positive feedback. Make a point of acknowledging their successes in detail, even when those successes are small ones.

Take a moment to consider:

- **Have you been a boss who has had trouble with retention?**

- **Do you have team members who have quit and stayed and function as if they are dead people working?**

In a recent study by Accenture to uncover why employees quit their jobs, the reasons for their unhappiness are:

1. **They don't like their boss (31%),**

2. **A lack of empowerment (31%),**

3. **Internal politics (35%) and**

4. **Lack of recognition (43%).**

PLEASE NOTE: The following exercise is by far the longest in the whole program, but it is the MOST IMPORTANT. Take the time to read or watch the "Creative Recognitions" fable and character descriptions as it sets you up for success in the program.

EXERCISE 1: Open to Experiencing Yourself and Others at Work

Read the illustrative fable "Creative Recognitions" in *The Positivity Pulse: Transforming Your Workplace* or go to **YouTube,** Creative Recognitions Inc., Narrative to listen to the narrated versions and watch the "Creative Recognitions" video and determine with whom you identify most closely in the illustrative fable about caterpillars and butterflies.

Next, review the qualities of the individual characters listed:

Frontline Worker Isabella

Coming to work is a joy for Isabella. She seems to be smiling from the inside out and anyone can tell she is flourishing in her job. She feels supported and appreciated. She understands work is a place she can grow and change in a positive way. Even as a frontline worker, she understands that the role she fills is just as important as that of the company's CEO because she represents the company to everyone she deals with daily. Even if occasionally she makes mistakes, after all, no one is perfect, there is no fallout and no drama. She doesn't waste time dwelling on what went wrong. Instead, she tries to learn from her mistakes and quickly steps back into the greatness of who she is.

Frontline Worker Justice

When Justice makes the effort to do well, he goes through his day hearing either nothing at all or comments such as "Thanks!" or "Good job!" but he never quite understands why he's being thanked or how he's doing a good job. At the end of each day, he feels as though he's had nothing but junk food to eat—he's had plenty of seemingly positive "nourishment" and reinforcement, but he craves more. He never quite feels satiated.

On the other hand, even for smaller infractions of policy or rules, he is given lots of negative attention. Sometimes the higher-ups even call a big meeting to discuss his rule breaking. Justice feels picked on by his supervisors. Although getting in trouble feels terrible, Justice continues to break the rules, or to walking that fine line between rules followed and rules broken.

Justice sometimes just seems to be going through the motions of working at his job. He becomes fearful that he won't meet his deadlines or that he may not survive a round of layoffs, should that happen. Sometimes Justice wonders why he even bothers to come to work. He works just as hard as Isabella and his accomplishments are similar to hers, but for some reason she is usually happy and seems to be changing and growing—even transforming. It also seems that she is more liked than Justice. "It's just not fair," Justice grumbles.

Team Chrysalis

Mr. Moody, Mrs. Crabtree, and Mr. Silencio, who supervise Justice and others like him, are members of Team Chrysalis. These leaders have diverse qualities and strengths. Some are new team players and some are seasoned. Their management styles are well established, but each is stuck in a unique way. Each encounters different kinds of obstacles to imparting their wisdom and greatness to the people in their lives.

Mr. Moody

Mr. Moody is a seasoned member of this team. He's close to retirement and has contributed in magnificent ways to the company's sustainable development. Although he regularly thanks his team members and frontline workers for doing a good job, his moods can sometimes make him difficult to get along with. He himself has tons of management experience, but for some reason he seems stuck—he has not moved far enough into his own potential to set a truly inspiring example for Justice, Isabella, and their co-workers.

Mrs. Crabtree

Mrs. Crabtree is task oriented and full of wisdom. But in her role as a team leader, she seems to spend much of the day barking orders and punishing her staff. She has a tendency to lecture when someone does something wrong. Even on a good day, she's abrupt and a bit crabby; she's in a constant state of frustration because she sees all around her only employees who are making mistakes! She can't seem to escalate disciplinary actions far enough to have an impact. At the same time, she doesn't ever seem to notice when her fellow team members or frontline workers are shining.

"That's just what I expect from them," she'd likely say if someone asked her why she never gave positive feedback to her team. "They're going to have to do a lot better than this to get a pat on the back from me. Besides, they get a paycheck to do what they were hired to do."

In private moments, Mrs. Crabtree feels unhappy that she can't seem to get her employees to perform better. She means well, but wonders why she doesn't feel as if she is flourishing at work or reaching her full potential. Like Mr. Moody, she knows that she isn't setting a great example for her fellow leaders or for the followers who count on her for guidance—but she doesn't know how to change to set this example.

Mr. Silencio

Mr. Silencio is the quiet type, but his contributions to the team are nothing less than stellar. He has studied lots of management theory and prides himself on understanding employees, but he has trouble implementing what he has learned for their benefit or expressing himself to them.

Although frontline workers and fellow team members learn a great deal from his intellect, he says barely a word to them directly. Whether they're doing well (which gives him a good feeling) or breaking the rules (which bothers him), he says nothing. His frontline workers have no trouble getting away with rule breaking when he is around. On the other hand, they don't feel inspired to do a better job, because Mr. Silencio doesn't seem to have a preference or a voice one way or the other. He is stuck in his own thoughts.

MODULE 1

The Nurtured Heart® Warriors Team

Mr. Kodak, Mrs. Polaroid, and Ms. Canon, members of the Nurtured Heart® Warriors Team, believe that creating a brilliant workplace is all about celebrating what's going well. They do not agree with top-down leadership styles, choosing instead to value the voice of every single person who works for the company. Their mission is to nurture personal and professional development—to support everyone in their transformation to greatness. Their transformation into effective leaders is complete, and they're ready to show others the way.

Mr. Kodak

Mr. Kodak seems to notice everything that's going right. Whomever he speaks to goes away feeling special. Even if it's something small—a choice to follow the rules, or just showing up and paying attention—he has something good to say about it. Practically everywhere he goes, Mr. Kodak takes "snapshots" of successes, both miniscule and massive, and he's unfailingly generous when giving feedback to team members about those successes.

Mrs. Polaroid

As a more seasoned manager, Mrs. Polaroid can keep up with Mr. Kodak in terms of noticing and acknowledging success. Like a Polaroid camera, she captures successes as they happen, then deepens that image of success by clearly stating how those successes reveal strengths and virtues. Her unique, intense style of relentlessly recognizing others takes some getting used to, but in the end, this ability to hone in on what's going right—and on what's so right about it—makes her an invaluable member of the management team.

Ms. Canon

Ms. Canon is the team's ultimate policy implementer and relentless rule follower, but she's not one to lecture, reprimand, or scold when rules are broken. Instead, she recognizes rule following. She keeps the team in full compliance by offering frequent reminders to those staying on task: you are wonderful for not breaking rules and for following policy. Ms. Canon appreciates team members for their willingness to change old habits, for staying in healthy control and for re-routing themselves back to compliance when they break rules or fail to comply with company policies and procedures. She's firm and strict, but also compassionate, loving, and proactive.

CEO Senora Corazon

Senora Corazon has been accused of wearing rose-colored glasses. She seems to believe, sometimes beyond reason, that all people can flourish. Her view is that giving recognition for every success, brilliance, and accomplishment is good for everyone, including the one who gives that recognition. She loves to notice what people are doing in the moment—or even what they're wearing!—and to take time to tell them what she's observing. She communicates to her people that she values them for their positive attitude and great work ethic.

Even when staff members seem to be having a rough day, she finds ways to positively acknowledge them for their ability to deal with hard times or difficult tasks. Other leaders have not agreed with her approach. They stand behind traditional ways of ruling over workers with enforced disciplinary action. This doesn't feel right to Senora Corazon

Senora Corazon is especially magnificent at bringing frontline workers back into balance when necessary. While she doesn't always hit the mark, she responds to her own errors and negative thoughts by redirecting her focus to what's great and right in the moment. Like the Nurtured Heart® Warriors Team, Senora Corazon has blossomed into a brilliant leader—and she's the most brilliant of them all.

WORKSHEET #1 : Module 1

POSITIVITY
PULSE
FOR **ORGANIZATIONS**

Worksheet #1: *"How Do I Experience Myself?"*   Date: _____

Answer the following questions:

1. Which Creative Recognitions, Inc. character do you currently identify most with and why?

   _____

   _____

2. What words describe your thoughts or feelings after reading the illustrative tale?

   _____

   _____

3. What is the main message that you drew from this tale?

   _____

   _____

4. Which Creative Recognitions, Inc. character would you choose to be more like and why?

   _____

   _____

5. Has reading this tale influenced the way you see, think, and/or feel about positive verses negative communications and attitudes at work?

   _____

   _____

6. In your workplace, do you tend to look for the positive and the greatness in people and situations? Or do you tend to look for what is wrong or complain about it, or do you ignore what is wrong, or blame others or judge them negatively? Explain and use some examples.

   _____

   _____

Set an Intention

- It is important to know what you want before you can take action to make it happen. Otherwise, without knowing clearly what you want, you can't determine the first step to getting started.

- Intention is one of the most powerful forces in life you can harness. Without a clear intention, you can wander around without meaning or direction. But once you find clarity of intention, you can set your stake in the ground and chart a clear course around it, and all the forces in the universe will seem to align to make even the most impossible possible.

- Sometimes in the early stage of imagining what you want you might have only a vague idea or desire. If you desire clarity but are having a difficult time figuring out what that is—don't worry. You might even feel you can't find a solid idea or a direction to latch onto. Some people describe it as a feeling of swimming around in a deep pot of soup. This "swimming in the soup" can actually be very useful. In fact, some people find they must spend time in this stage of imagining while they are trying to find clarity or while they are exploring different options. But be aware that a pattern of remaining vague after evidence or options are weighed can sabotage your forward motion of change, leading to confusion, inertia, and stagnation. A pattern of vagueness or indecision may even be an attempt to control the situation by not setting a clear intention or taking action.

- An intention can be long-term or short-term. It can be something for everyday or even every moment. It can be about something in particular or about a quality in life or a way of being. Whatever your intention may be, it is important to state it so that you can focus your attention, take action, and measure your success.

- When you set and state an intention, you are making it clear to yourself and others what you want to do.

WORKSHEET #2: Module 1

POSITIVITY
PULSE
FOR **ORGANIZATIONS**

Worksheet #2: *"Positivity and Intention"*   Date: _____

Answer the following questions:

1. On a scale of 1 to 10, 10 being the most positive and joyous work atmosphere you can imagine, what number do you give to the positivity of your workplace culture?

   _____

   Using the above scale, what number do you give yourself?

   _____

2. If you rated the positivity of your workplace culture less than 10, what effect do you feel that has on your overall morale and satisfaction with your job?

   _____

   _____

   And for yourself?

   _____

   _____

3. If your overall workplace positivity were to increase significantly, what benefits would you gain?

   _____

   _____

4. If you increased your positivity, what benefits do you think or feel you would experience?

   _____

   _____

The 7 Steps To Ignite Flourishing In Leaders, Teams And Organizations

5. Do your interactions with others get you the results you want?

_____

_____

6. Where do you want to be when you come to the end of this program? For example: I intend to learn how to communicate more effectively or I intend to feel more positively connected to people at work or I intend to actively appreciate others more frequently.

_____

_____

7. What would you have to do, change, or give up to make your intention possible?

_____

_____

8. What are some of the benefits you would receive as a result of living your intention?

_____

_____

Insert your intention from Number 6 here for easy reference:

_____

_____

_____

_____

W O R K S H E E T # 2

JOURNAL: Module 1

Journal for Clarity and Understanding

You might be familiar with the practice of journaling. Some people have a regular practice of recording and exploring their thoughts and experiences in a physical journal or in an online program.

Journaling is especially helpful if you are exploring new ideas, looking for clarity, or want to deepen your understanding. The idea is to get more in touch with your feelings and thoughts by taking the time to let them develop and flow.

There will be occasional journal pages throughout the modules. They are for you. You can choose to share them or keep them private. You might even choose to keep a separate personal journal as you work through the program.

Here are a few helpful hints on how to journal:

- **Find a quiet time and place where you are comfortable and select your favorite writing instruments or computer device. You may even want to have a dedicated notebook to write your private musings.**

- **Take some deep breaths in through your nose and out through your mouth and ponder the question or feelings you want to explore. Then write what you are thinking and feeling.**

- **Allow yourself to tap into your intuition and creativity. Some people experience a deeper emotional connection to feelings when they write and others when they type.**

- **Let the words flow, letting whatever you are experiencing come out and onto the surface without editing or judging what you write or draw.**

Journaling provides you with an opportunity to explore and understand yourself better and to get clarity about things you may be feeling. You can create and write/draw anything you desire. Journaling is for your benefit and can be a private practice. It is up to you to decide if you want to share it with anyone.

WORKSHEET #3: *"My Positivity"* Journal   Date: _____

Using your new knowledge and intention, describe your ideal positive self at work, full of nurturing communications and energy. Paint or describe a colorful picture for yourself. Imagine scenes throughout your whole day. What old habits and ways of communicating would you like to release? What new habits and ways of communicating would bring you more joy throughout the day? Release your fears, judgments, and limitations as you imagine how things would change if you consistently received and delivered heartfelt positive recognition and appreciation.

_____

_____

_____

_____

_____

_____

_____

_____

_____

_____

_____

_____

_____

_____

_____

_____

_____

_____

W
O
R
K
S
H
E
E
T

J
O
U
R
N
A
L

#

3

ACTION STEPS: Module 1

ACTION STEP 1: Determine and write at least one thing you could change your attitude about by choosing to see what is strong and good about the person/situation instead of what is wrong.

_____

_____

_____

_____

ACTION STEP 2: Choose two to three people who you interact with at work and focus on giving them some positive recognition this week. Write their names here and what is strong about them that you will recognize.

_____

_____

_____

_____

ACTION STEP 3: What is a step you can take TODAY to create change and make your Positivity Pulse begin to beat more strongly in your workplace?

_____

_____

_____

_____

The 7 Steps To Ignite Flourishing In Leaders, Teams And Organizations

Answer the following questions:

1. What did you set out to do by starting this module?

_____

_____

_____

2. What did you accomplish?

_____

_____

_____

3. What do you need to change to be the person you want to be?

_____

_____

_____

4. ⬤ What is the Pearl of Positivity Wisdom you received this week?

_____

_____

_____

5. What is your Action Step **WOWEE** (Within One Week to Energize and Excel) intention you will commit to for this upcoming week?

_____

_____

_____

A
S
S
E
S
S
M
E
N
T

M
O
D
U
L
E

#

1

IGNITE

"You become what you think about."

~ Earl Nightingale, author

NOTES

IGNITE

MODULE 2

Positivity
The Science of Happiness at Work

If, after working through Module 1, you are still wondering why you should be at all concerned about increasing your own positivity and happiness or creating a positive environment at work for your employees, in this module you'll discover some recent science that just might shock you. (Hint: Employers tend to value happiness and positive work environments much less than employees do.) We'll also look at some of the consequences of negative environments that are highlighted in studies, as well as how you can learn to unlock positivity and reap its benefits.

Even though the idea of positive psychology is spreading like wildfire in many areas, some people hearing about the "new" ideas of happiness and positivity at work still consider those ideas to be trendy or dismiss them as rather "fluffy" and unnecessary for their workplace. Read on and you'll see why that attitude could be a costly mistake.

Module 2 Objectives

- To introduce the impact and importance of cultivating happiness at work.

- To discover happiness at work is a mindset that can be developed and measured.

- To see how nurturing more positivity at work can affect the bottom line.

- To learn how tweaking just a few things each day can affect your personal outcomes.

MODULE 2

Module 2 Summary

- Being happy at work contributes to increased productivity and makes good business sense. (Pryce-Jones)

- Increasing the 5Cs, which are the important drivers to happiness: Contribution, Conviction, Culture, Commitment and Confidence, builds happiness at work. When one falls, the others become unstable. (Pryce-Jones, 2010)

- Trust, Recognition and Pride support the 5Cs and are the fundamental building blocks in any organization. (Pryce-Jones, 2010)

- You can steadily increase your happiness by increasing your positivity ratio every day. (Fredrickson, 2009)

- Moment by moment, bit by bit, day by day, you build the flourishing life you want.

- **Investing in Human Capital by increasing Psychological and Social Capital = Improved Workplace Relations and Increased Productivity. HC(PC x SC) = IWR + $$$**

Calls for a Paradigm Shift

Over the past number of years, there has been an increasingly vociferous call for a specific paradigm shift in the workplace. The call: to shift away from top-down, autocratic styles of leading into modes that are more about service and leadership from the heart, more collaborative, and more engaging for all, or in other words, modes that are more positive. Ken Blanchard, Jackie and Kevin Freiberg, Barbara Fredrickson, Martin Seligman, and Jessica Pryce-Jones are all names you might recognize as being devoted to this paradigm change.

While it is true large companies and their many layers of bureaucracy have a difficult time changing their internal structure and culture, the numbers evidenced in research and exit polls continue to demand a change in the status quo if companies want to keep their employees happy, productive, and loyal.

On the one hand, change is difficult for many individuals, and even more so for very large organizations. On the other hand, nothing is constant but change, and those who fail to change are outmoded sooner or later.

Let's take a look at some shocking numbers that support the call for creating a new style of leadership from the heart, a style that is about being of service *to* employees rather than demanding one-way service *from* them. Please visit **www.PositivityPulse.com**.

Consequences of not increasing positivity at work:

- A recent survey shows 65% of people who quit don't quit their job—they quit their boss.

- The least happy employees spend only 40% of their time being productive at work. This means the unhappiest employees are really only working two days a week even though they are physically there for five days. (iOpener, 2010)

- Unhappy employees are currently intending to stay in their jobs for about 36 months. Before the Great Recession they intended to move on in approximately six months, but now you get to have their unhappy and underperforming influence for a lot longer. (iOpener, 2010)

- Unhappy employees have also lost up to a third of their self-confidence, resilience, motivation, goal achievement, engagement, pride, trust, recognition, and the feeling that they are achieving their potential. This directly results in negative effects on project delivery, ideas, delivery of new products, and acceptance of and adaptation to change. (iOpener, 2010)

- Of the top 10 reasons why employees quit, according to exit interviews conducted by Price Waterhouse (of 19,000+ people) for their clients, only 12% cited compensation issues. The rest of the issues had to do with supervisor issues, recognition, opportunity for growth, and advancement and fairness issues, to name a few. (Witt, 2012)

While most employers would mistakenly tell you 9 out of 10 people who quit a company do so for compensation reasons, these studies and others show that when employees are not getting their needs met, they tend to check out by giving as little effort as they can get by with before they eventually move on. (Witt 2012) We call those "dead people working." In other words, they may still be physically there, but mentally and emotionally they have checked out. This is not only bad for them, but is devastating for the business bottom line, as they are unproductive at best and quite disruptive at their worst.

WORKSHEET #4: Module 2

Worksheet #4: *"At My Work..."*   Date: _____

Answer the following questions:

Wondering if you feel happy at work? Here are some questions to ask yourself about your overall satisfaction at work.

1. I feel my employer cares about my happiness and provides me with a positive and healthy work environment.

   _____

2. I feel seen and appreciated at work and feel like I "fit in."

   _____

3. I feel valued at work and that my contributions as a team member are important.

   _____

4. I receive positive feedback on my performance quite often.

   _____

5. I am committed to giving my best efforts at work because I believe my organization treats me fairly.

   _____

6. I take pride in my work and I can see how my work contributes to the success of the organization.

   _____

7. I support the values of my organization and I take pride in being a part of my organization.

   _____

The 7 Steps To Ignite Flourishing In Leaders, Teams And Organizations

How Happiness at Work Impacts the Bottom Line

Building happiness at work generates revenue by increasing performance and productivity and it cuts costs by enabling employees to improve efficiency. (iOpener, 2013)

We see The Science of Happiness as a formula that succinctly expresses this:

Investing in Human Capital by increasing Psychological and Social Capital = Improved Workplace Relations and Increased Productivity HC(PC x SC) = IWR + $$$

Let's see actual findings that support the formula:

In an organization of 1,000 employees, increasing happiness at work benefited the bottom line by:

- 46% reduction in the cost of employee turnover.

- 19% reduction the cost of sick leave.

- 12% increase in performance and productivity.

Organizations embrace the science of happiness at work because it has such a dramatic effect on overall business results, leaders, and employees. (iOpener, 2013)

The Science of Happiness at Work Defined

The Science of Happiness at Work is a mindset that enables action to maximize performance and achieve potential. Positive emotions indicate the actions are on the right track but mindset matters most. This mindset results in positive attitude, optimism, resilience and courage, or, in other words, psychological capital.

Psychological capital is an essential part of social capital, which in turn contributes greatly to human capital and that of course affects the bottom line. What's exciting about this new science is that there really is strong data showing just how clear the financial benefits are that support the science of happiness at work.

In a five year research program in which Jessica Pryce-Jones compared and contrasted the happiest employees against their unhappiest colleagues, she found that organizations benefited from the happiest employees because the happiest employees:

- Are 47% more productive.

- Intend to stay longer in their jobs (regardless of recession).

- Take 300% less sick leave.

And employees who were happy at work versus the unhappiest benefited in the following ways:

- Are 180% more energized.

- Experience 155% more happiness in their jobs.

- Perceive they are 150% happier with life.

- Find 108% more engagement.

- Feel 50% more motivated.

- Find 50% more belief in their potential.

- Are 40% more confident.

- Think they have 35% more control over what they do. (Pryce-Jones, 2010)

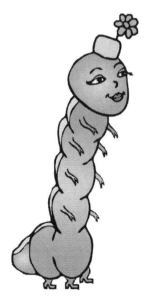

So What Does the Science of Happiness at Work Consist of?

Happiness at work is driven by the 5Cs and is supported by trust, recognition, and pride.

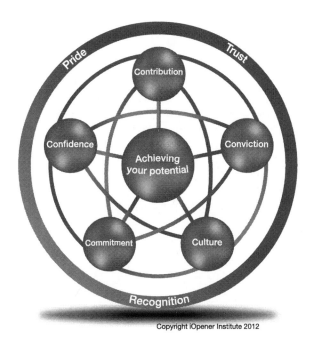

Copyright iOpener Institute 2012

The 5Cs

Jessica Pryce-Jones' research has identified five components (5Cs) that inform and build happiness at work:

- *Contribution* **is the effort an individual or team makes.**
- *Conviction* **is short-term motivation.**
- *Culture* **is a feeling of fitting in at work.**
- *Commitment* **is long-term engagement.**
- *Confidence* **is the belief in one's abilities.**

The 5Cs form an ecosystem, which works together to drive performance. But when individuals, teams, and organizations have high levels of all the 5Cs coupled with trust, recognition, and pride, then they will perform at their best whatever happens. Read on to learn how you can measure and increase your happiness. (Pryce-Jones, 2010)

MODULE 2

Trust, Recognition, and Pride

The 5Cs are supported by trust, recognition, and pride. They correlate with each component of happiness at work, and are fundamental building blocks of any successful organization. Here's more about them:

- **Trust in your organization flows from two sources: your colleagues and your senior leaders.**

- **Recognition from your organization encompasses what you are, what you're doing, and how you do it.**

- **Pride in your organization comes from identifying with it, achieving success, and being aware of your colleagues' success too. (Pryce-Jones, 2010)**

Worksheet #5: *"How Happy Am I at Work?"*   Date: _____

Look back at the explanations on the prior two pages. Give yourself a score from 0-10 (0 is the lowest and 10 is the highest) for each variable listed. Be honest. Your rating is based on how much you believe, sense or feel these variables are present at work for you.

A. Fill in your scores below:

The 5Cs	Your Score	Average
Conviction		
Contribution		
Culture		
Commitment		
Confidence		

Trust		
Pride		
Recognition		

B. Answer the following questions:

1. **Which of the 5Cs did you score highest in? Were you surprised by the result? Why or why not?**

   _____

   _____

2. **Which was the lowest? Were you surprised by the result? Why or why not?**

   _____

   _____

POSITIVITY PULSE
FOR ORGANIZATIONS

3. What do you think you need to keep doing in order to sustain your highest "C"?

_____

_____

4. What are your thoughts on how to increase your lowest "C"?

_____

_____

5. Did the results raise your awareness regarding your happiness level at work or did it confirm what you already energetically felt or believed? Explain.

_____

_____

6. Trust. Recognition. Pride. What do your results reveal to you beyond the numeric value? Trust is a pinnacle for optimized relationships. Feeling a sense of pride helps you find meaning in your work and being recognized for your contributions builds trust and pride. What are your thoughts about this?

_____

_____

7. Are you aware that your happiness level at work can impact you negatively at home and in your personal life? If so, what is your experience? Does knowing this fact stimulate you to acquire more happiness at work?

_____

_____

* Sherry Blair is a licensed practitioner through the iOpener Institute under the United States Global Partner.

** The iPPQ measures individuals, teams and entire organizations and can be utilized as a developmental tool to increase happiness at work as well as a method for tracking the progress.

W O R K S H E E T # 5

"Happiness at work is a mindset that allows you to maximize performance and achieve your potential. You do this by being mindful of the highs and lows when working alone or with others."

~ Jessica Pryce Jones, CEO
iOpener Institute for People & Performance

Positivity

Now that you have a base-line measurement of your happiness at work, lets dive in to a related but slightly different concept that we will be working with to "ignite flourishing" in leaders, teams, and organizations. Increasing positive emotions is the "how" to increasing happiness to the level of flourishing.

Barbara Fredrickson's decades long research on her Broaden and Build theory of positivity has already proven that:

Positivity broadens your mind and yields these results:

- **Calls forth more possibilities within us**

- **Increases your scope of attention**

- **Increases creativity on verbal tasks**

- **Betters clinical reasoning**

- **Helps to see more solutions in and be better able to cope with adversity**

- **Causes managers to be more effective interpersonally**

- **Causes managers to infect their work groups with more positivity which leads to better coordination among team members and reduces effort to get work done**

Builds your best future by building:

- Psychological strength

- Good mental habits

- Social connections

- Physical health

- Transforming you for the better

Fuels your resilience by:

- Allowing for faster recovery from anticipated negativity

- Reducing time spent worrying during adversity

- Increases amount of hope

- Reframing bad events as opportunities

- Adopting a wait-and-see attitude about future threats

- Creating greater openness that dissolves negativity faster

- Allowing your heart and mind to become more fully open to connect with caring others (Fredrickson, 2009)

"The effects of positivity are not random. They are predictable and sweeping. Your life is a complex tapestry of your psychological strengths, mental habits, social connections, physical health, and more. In the span of three months, positivity can change these various parts of you in beautiful synchrony. At a deep level, positivity can change who you are. And those changes can make life itself more fulfilling."

~ Barbara Fredrickson

POSITIVITY
PULSE
FOR ORGANIZATIONS

 KEYS TO SUCCESS ——————————

Three things you can do regularly to increase your positivity:

- Count your blessings.
- Keep a daily tally of kind things you do for others.
- Connect with others.

Now discover how positivity and negativity work together to tip your life toward flourishing.

The Positivity Ratios

Fredrickson's Positivity Ratios formulas allow us to determine as a ratio our positive versus negative emotional experiences over a given time period. To do this, take the number of your positive emotional experiences divided by the number of negative emotional experiences in a given day to find a ratio.

Positivity Ratios (P/N)
- **Pathology (such as depression): P/N < 1 – to – 1**
- **Languishing: P/N ~ 2 – to – 1**
- **Flourishing: P/N > 3 – to – 1**
(Fredrickson 2013)

Sadly, 80% of Americans fall short of the P/N > 3-to-1 positivity ratio that predicts flourishing health. (Fredrickson, 2013) But luckily you can use the tools in this Action Guide to increase your positivity ratio and create a more positive, healthier, vibrant and flourishing life!

Looking at the Positivity Ratios formulas, you can see positive emotions play a unique role in achieving and promoting flourishing: ratios above 3:1 lead to greater flourishing. And the

Flourishing Positivity Ratio becomes even more meaningful when we define flourishing as a multidimensional combination of:

- Feeling good (hedonic well-being) which is feeling satisfied with life and having pleasant affect

  PLUS

- Doing good (eudaimonic well-being) including such things as sense of purpose and meaning, generativity and contribution, and growth as well as resilience and social integration. (Fredrickson, 2009) (Keyes, 2002) and (Fredrickson & Losada, 2005, pg. 678).

Daily experiences of positive emotions predict and produce growth in personal resources such as competence, meaning and purpose in life, optimism, resilience, self-acceptance and positive relationships, as well as physical health. In other words, feeling good *drives* optimal functioning by building the enduring personal resources you need to see new possibilities, bounce back from setbacks, connect more deeply with others and become the best version of yourself. (Cohn et al., 2009, Fredrickson et al., 2008; Kok et al., 2013)

People that flourish thrive because they tend to experience greater positive emotional reactivity, i.e. more positive enjoyment and energy in response to everyday pleasant routine activities. They also experience bigger "boosts" in positivity in response to routine daily events such as helping others, interactivity, playing, learning and engaging in spiritual activities. (Catalino and Fredrickson, 2011).

Over time, flourishers' greater positive emotional reactivity predicted their growth in personal resources which in turn predicted their higher levels of flourishing. In other words, their flourishing ignited the spiral of more positivity.

The Role of Negativity

What has already been discovered is that measure for measure bad, as in negativity, is stronger than good, as in positivity. More than you perhaps realize, your positivity ratio depends on your daily diet of negativity.

Fredrickson tells us that in order to live your best life, to flourish, the goal is to reduce inappropriate or gratuitous negativity, which is neither helpful nor healthy. The first step is

awareness that you are starting a downward spiral of negative thinking, and then taking steps to stop it.

The goal is to reduce negativity, not to eliminate it. You are not trying to be positive and happy 100% of the time. First of all, given the full range of human emotions, how would you know when you were happy if there was nothing to compare it with? Secondly, some negative emotions have their place and are appropriate and useful, such as grief and loss, anger at injustices, standing up with anger against injustices, fear of things that could hurt us or our loved ones, etc. And thirdly, extremely high levels of positive emotions that are heightened, persistent, and often contextually inappropriate and unmitigated by negative emotions could be indicative of mental instability or mental illness. (Gruber, 2011).

You can learn to tell the difference between necessary negativity and gratuitous negativity. Necessary negativity makes us aware of facts we need to face and deal with. When faced with necessary negativity we are free to make a decision whether action is needed or not. On the other hand, gratuitous negativity doesn't do us any good and often becomes blown way out of proportion and keeps us ruminating for way too long. (Fredrickson, 2009)

KEYS TO SUCCESS

To Reduce Inappropriate or Gratuitous Negative Thinking:

- Train yourself to recognize when you are starting to have negative thoughts.

- Have a list of healthy distractions that will take your mind off your negativity such as taking a walk, practicing a hobby, reaching out to a friend for a positive shared experience, working on a task you've been meaning to get to, reading a good book, etc.

- Dispute negative thinking by asking yourself a few questions and examining the facts. What set you off or triggered your negative thoughts or beliefs? How did they make you feel? What are the facts? Keep asking yourself questions until you can dissolve the negative thoughts.

- Keep asking: "And *then* what is the worst that can happen?" until you dissolve the negative thoughts and beliefs.

Dealing with People with Negative Behavior

Fredrickson gives some great advice on how to deal with these situations.

- Modify the social situation: alter the typical situations in which you interact with the person. Be honest with yourself to see if there is something that you do, like have negative reactions or make negative remarks or assumptions.

- Attend differently: even though the person might have some qualities you find distasteful, choose instead to see what is positive about him or her.

- Change meanings: could this person or situation be a teacher in disguise? Is this something that will keep coming up until you take action to deal with it? (Fredrickson, 2009)

Thinking of a Person with Whom You Have Negative Interactions:

1. In what ways could you modify the social situation?

   _____

2. Is there something you do that contributes to the negativity, like being sarcastic or rolling your eyes? Think and name it if you can.

   _____

3. What positive qualities about him or her can you choose to see or appreciate?

   _____

4. Is this person possibly a mirror that reflects qualities you don't like about yourself?

   _____

5. Is there some issue that will keep resurfacing until you take action to deal with it?

   _____

KEYS TO SUCCESS

The consistency of flourishing positivity ratios measuring above 3 to 1 discovered independently by other researchers in different fields is extraordinary and worth your attention. John Gottman found flourishing marriages to have positivity ratios of about 5 to 1, whereas languishing and failed marriages had positivity ratios lower than 1 to 1. (Gottman and Silver, 1999) And clinical psychologist Robert Schwartz found optimal positivity ratios are about 4 to 1, compared to the "normal" positivity ratios of about 2 to 1, and those of depressed people are lower than 1 to 1. (Schwartz et al, 2002)

Happiness at Work

- Taking your happiness "temperature" at work reveals to you the range of your Inner Wealth™, or personal resources, that may be depleted, meaning that your reservoir is running low and action is required. Conversely, if your reservoir is full and flourishing, your action steps are designed toward sustaining those levels of happiness at work. **From a business perspective, this makes sound sense as the research reveals that productivity is strongly linked to happiness at work.**

- **Achieving your full potential** is at the heart of The Science of Happiness at Work map and increasing the 5Cs and trust, recognition, and pride is the "how" to make that happen. Achieving your full potential is strongly associated with feeling energized and applying your strengths and skills, learning new skills and overcoming challenges.

- Building from the inside-out is key and is consistent with achieving your goals: having clear objectives, bringing forth issues that are important to you, and feeling a sense of security at your job. Working from the inside-out, this is the heart of contribution and contribution is the most important component of happiness at work.

- While you can increase your personal resource of contribution, as a leader you also need to build the spirit of contribution from the **outside-in** by listening, providing positive

feedback, respecting the team members, and showing appreciation for the work they are doing.

- Stand your **conviction** by being grounded in knowing you are doing the right thing. The key elements for conviction are being motivated, which involves purpose, direction, and effort, and is enhanced by having a choice, competence, and connectedness. Efficiency and effectiveness are also constituents of conviction with being effective rising to a higher level of what matters most. They too require positive energy to stay on your A-game.

- Be mindful of how your energy contributes to the **culture** of your organization. To do this go deeper than the "skin-color" reflection of culture by being sure your organization's values are clearly stated and upheld and that you articulate them and operate from those values. Understand what it takes for you to relish your job, project sincere general liking and mutual respect for your colleagues, build a strong workplace character, and maintain a level of autonomy over your daily activities.

- You increase your sense of **commitment** when you believe you are doing something worthwhile and are interested in your job. When you believe in the vision of the organization and experience strong bursts of positive emotion, you feel more committed. All these feelings and beliefs are interactive and reinforce one another.

- **Confidence** is increased when you get things done, acquire high levels of self-belief, and understand your roles backward and forward.

- **Pride, trust, and recognition** are intertwined like strands in your psychological "DNA." They clearly are strongly mapped onto all the 5Cs for overall happiness at work. Pride emerges when you identify with your organization, comprehend your level of contribution, know whom your work affects and are aware of the wider impact. Trust flows from your colleagues and senior leaders but is reciprocal and is a two-way street so remember your responsibility in recognizing and honoring those around you! (Pryce-Jones, 2010)

KEYS TO SUCCESS

Investing in Human Capital by increasing Psychological and Social Capital = Improved Workplace Relations and Increased Productivity which benefits the bottom line HC(PC x SC) = IWR + $$$

ACTION STEP 1: Make a list of several positive and healthy activities you can do to distract yourself whenever you start to dwell on an unnecessary negative situation.

_____

_____

_____

_____

ACTION STEP 2: List at least one negative thing that you tend to ruminate on and what you will do to distract yourself when you find you are starting to think about it.

_____

_____

_____

_____

ACTION STEP 3: At the end of each workday, write several things you are grateful for or that you noticed went well if feeling grateful does not apply.

_____

_____

_____

_____

ASSESSMENT: Module 2

Answer the following questions:

1. **What did you set out to do by starting this module?**

   _____

   _____

   _____

2. **What did you accomplish?**

   _____

   _____

   _____

3. **What do you need to change to be the person you want to be?**

   _____

   _____

   _____

4. **What is the Pearl of Positivity Wisdom you received this week?**

   _____

   _____

   _____

5. **What is your Action Step WOWEE (Within One Week to Energize and Excel) intention you will commit to for this upcoming week?**

   _____

   _____

   _____

A S S E S S M E N T   M O D U L E   # 2

48

"Let us be grateful to people who make us happy, they are the charming gardeners who make our souls blossom."

~ Marcel Proust

NOTES

IGNITE

MODULE 3

Build
Nurtured Heart® Foundations

Flourishing at work is all about cultivating wealth in relationships. Module 1 has opened your awareness to different styles of relating and how positivity and negativity in relationships impacts us. Module 2 illuminates why positivity and happiness at work is important and the benefits they bring.

In Module 3, you will discover the four key concepts that are the foundation for building a Positivity Pulse in your relationships. As you read the stories let yourself think about how you can transfer your understanding to situations at work. Doing the exercises will help you build your skills.

Module 3 Objectives

- To learn the Four Foundational Concepts that support the Nurtured Heart Approach®. (Glasser, Bowdidge, and Bravo, 2007)

- To understand how to apply the concepts in relationships.

Module 3 Summary

- Leaders are their employees' favorite toys.

- Remember Baby Steps to create success.

- The Toll Taker teaches us we get to choose how we see things.

- Game Theory shows us clear rules and clear consequences.

"If we commit to harnessing the power of games for real happiness and real change, then a better reality is more than possible—it is likely. And in that case, our future together will be quite extraordinary."

~ **Jane McGonical, Reality is Broken: Why Games Make Us Better and How They Can Change the World**

The Four Foundational Concepts

Foundational Concept I

Leaders are their employees' favorite toys.

As odd as that sounds, it's true. Think about it. As infants we come into this world "wired" to learn how to conduct ourselves in the world from the responses we get from our parents or caregivers. Those parents or caregivers are our absolute favorite toys because no other toys can match what they do. The countless emotions, expressions, and energies in response to our behavior, good or bad, teach us how to get the greatest possible attention, validation and reinforcement from adults.

As social beings, as we grow we continue to require love and attention to thrive—and not only from friends, partners, and family members. This need extends to the workplace, and because leaders have an authoritative role there, they become the employees' new "favorite toys."

Module 2 taught that in the past few years, a great deal of research in industrial and organizational psychology and positive psychology speaks to the validity of positive relationship in the workplace. This research demonstrates that the primary motivation to excel at work and cultivate good relationships is not financial. Having a voice, feeling valued, appreciated, and connected are the real key factors that inspire team members to participate at their highest level. Employees are constantly looking to leadership for appreciation, feedback, support, and reinforcement in the form of energy and attention. In this way, leaders can think of themselves as "toys" from which team members want to get as much positive and energized relationship as possible.

Employees make choices based in large part on their desire to see leaders light up in response to those choices. For some, bad choices get made out of the sheer desire to get *some* kind

of reaction from this favorite toy, because success doesn't seem to make the toy's bells and whistles go off in any reliable sort of way.

When team leaders find ways to see, appreciate, and verbally acknowledge success—to *energize* success—team members come to understand their favorite toys will predictably light up and make fun sounds in response to their good choices. This positive attention is reinforcement of their good choices and success and leads them to give their best.

KEYS TO SUCCESS

Find ways to give positive energy, response, and relationship for the good stuff, just like Senora Corazon and the Nurtured Heart® Warriors Team.

JOURNAL WORKSHEET: Module 3

WORKSHEET #6: *"My Favorite Toy"* **Journal**   Date: _____

Write about a current or past team leader or boss or other work relationship in your life. On a scale of 1 to 10, 10 being the most "lit up," how easy was it for you to get their "bells and whistles" going? Did their reactions to your successes and/or mistakes encourage you to do your best? Describe how their reactions or lack thereof made you feel and what effect their reactions had on your desire to do your best.

_____

_____

_____

_____

_____

_____

_____

_____

_____

_____

_____

_____

_____

_____

_____

_____

_____

_____

_____

_____

WORKSHEET JOURNAL # 6

Foundational Concept II

Baby Steps: Catching Success and Goodness vs. Creating Success and Goodness

Baby Steps is a way for us to shape the behavior that we want to see by rewarding it. In Nurtured Heart® terms, we use recognitions and strategies and the big payoff is our connection, positive energy and most importantly, our relationship—we are the reward! For some employees, we have to look for the baby step progress along the way as we work to achieve goals that change behaviors. John Kotter, Konosuke Matsushita Professor of Leadership, Emeritus, at the Harvard Business School, a New York Times best-selling author, and the founder of Kotter International reminds us that it is essential to celebrate short-term wins in a change process. Failure to do so, can result in the doom of change initiatives.

As soon as we see any movement toward the desired behavior we wish to see, or the slightest positive outcome in performance and productivity, we shower the person, or team with plenty of energized rewards in the forms or our energy, our recognitions and when appropriate, with our affection. With consistent rewards, given each time, people soon learn to get those rewards by purposely showing the behavior we want to see, or by working hard to be a team player in a transformational change initiative. Once that connection is made, we see improved new positive behavior and less and less negative behavior until it may even disappear altogether!

This speaks to the importance of energizing, rewarding, and celebrating success every step of the way starting with you and toward others. It speaks to the importance of placing your attention on the Baby Steps of progress by celebrating the short-term wins along the way and finding ways to create success rather than standing by and waiting for it to happen. If we set our expectations too high and fail to notice ourselves and others moving toward a goal, even when we are not soaring and flying high, we miss infinite opportunities to nurture greatness. And if we bring negative energy into our daily lives and put ourselves or others down when we fail to soar to great heights of achievement we create an environment of negativity.

The Nurtured Heart Approach® gives us tools for seeing and acknowledging success, no matter what. Every time we the slightest baby step toward progress, success is created. The NHA teaches us to take every opportunity

to create successes that would otherwise not exist. If we find ways to honor ourselves and others for what isn't wrong, we have a whole lot more to celebrate.

> *"What do your people at work and your spouse and kids at home have in common with a five-ton killer whale? Probably a whole lot more than you think, according to top business consultant and mega-bestselling author Ken Blanchard and his coauthors from SeaWorld. In his moving and inspirational book, Whale Done, Blanchard explains that both whales and people perform better when you accentuate the positive. He shows how using the techniques of animal trainers—specifically those responsible for the killer whales of SeaWorld—can supercharge your effectiveness at work and at home."*
>
> *~ Free Press*

Worksheet #7: *"Baby Stepping"*   Date: _____

With this concept of Catching Success and Goodness vs. Creating Success and Goodness, reflect on a relationship you had with a key work manager or boss at some time in your work history and how it inspired you to do your best, or not, and how it affected you emotionally. It should be the most intense relationship you had, whether positive, neutral, or negative. Recall aspects of this relationship that affected your feelings and experience in your work life.

1. Did you look forward to going to work each day?

   _____

2. Did you feel "seen" and valued for your efforts?

   _____

3. What kind of feedback did you receive?

   _____

4. Were you encouraged or challenged to use your key strengths to figure out your duties or to advance?

   _____

5. Did you feel your "voice," opinions, or suggestions mattered?

   _____

6. Did you feel your contributions mattered?

   _____

7. Was it a supportive and collaborative environment or competitive and isolating?

   _____

8. Were your successes acknowledged and celebrated?

   _____

MODULE 3

KEYS TO SUCCESS

Reinforce and energize yourself and others for following rules; for showing good judgment; for living values like thoughtfulness, responsibility, respectfulness, creativity, conscientiousness, or generosity. Small successes lead to further success–before you know it, you are leaping with giant steps to ever-greater heights of energized success.

Worksheet #8: *"A Key Work Relationship Experience"*   Date: _____

Please answer the following questions, reflecting on what you wrote in *"My Favorite Toy"* and *"Baby Stepping"* Worksheet pages:

1. Reflecting back to your key work relationship, was there a single aspect of that relationship that stands out in your memory? Describe.

   _____

   _____

2. Knowing the "Favorite Toy" concept, and reflecting back on that work relationship, are you aware of any action you took, or didn't take, to get attention from your superior?

   _____

   _____

3. Again reflecting on your journaling and your new understanding, what additional kinds of attention could you have benefited from?

   _____

   _____

4. Did you feel reinforced and energized when you had even small successes?

   _____

   _____

5. Were your larger successes recognized and celebrated?

   _____

   _____

W
O
R
K
S
H
E
E
T
#
8

The Nurtured Heart Approach® teaches us to take every opportunity to create successes *that would otherwise not exist*. If we find ways to honor employees for what isn't wrong, we have a whole lot more to celebrate.

But wait! Celebrate what's *not* going wrong?

Create success that would otherwise *not* exist?

How does one do this without being a total Pollyanna, pink-washing the world until everything looks rosy and ignoring problems?

Consider the tale of the Toll Taker, the next foundational principle of the Nurtured Heart Approach®.

Foundational Concept III

Toll Taker: Choosing the Way We See Things

In his presentations and books, Howard Glasser shares an old story about a dancing Toll Taker on the San Francisco Bay Bridge. The professor who originally told Glasser this story reported that he had driven over to the dancer's lane to pay his toll. "It looks like you're having the time of your life," the professor told the Toll Taker. The Toll Taker replied, "Of course! I have the best job in the world and the best office in the world." He colorfully describes the beautiful views he drinks in daily. He gets to see sunrises and sunsets while on the job—and, as luck would have it, he's an aspiring dancer who gets paid to practice in his glass-walled office high above the water! When the professor inquires about the other Toll Takers who don't seem so energized, the dancing Toll Taker responds, "Oh, those guys in the stand-up coffins? They're no fun!"

We get to choose how we see things. The Toll Taker could have focused on the difficult aspects of his job: long days on his feet, car exhaust fumes, or disgruntled commuters. That's what the guys in the stand-up coffins are likely focusing on. He chooses, instead, to dwell on what's right about where he is and what he's doing. The best part about this story is that it teaches us that we get to make the choice of what we focus on or how we see things in any given moment of

the day. No matter how much we've dwelled on the negative in the past, each new moment is an opportunity to see and acknowledge what's right in our worlds and in those people around us.

Choosing to focus on what's right is about getting out of the way and allowing problems to solve themselves. By making this choice, we set intentions to climb to ever greater heights of success instead of wallowing in negativity.

KEYS TO SUCCESS

In an instant we can decide to see what's going strong, thereby changing our experience of the moment.

POSITIVITY PULSE FOR ORGANIZATIONS

Worksheet #9: *"I Choose the Way I See Things"*   Date: _____

What Do I Focus On In a Negative Way?	I Can Instead Choose to See What Is Strong About This Situation By:

W O R K S H E E T # 9

The Evidence is in...

In Module 2 you discovered many business related benefits of increasing positivity in the workplace. Just in case you might still be wondering why you should add a healthy dose of heartfelt positivity to your daily diet, below is a sampling of the scientific evidence (Fredrickson, 2009) that has been pouring in over the last few years linking positivity and health.

People's increased positivity predicts:

- Lower levels of stress-related hormones.

- Higher levels of growth-related hormones.

- Higher levels of bond-related hormones

- Higher level of dopamine.

- Higher levels of opioids.

- Enhanced immune system functioning.

- Diminished inflammatory responses to stress.

- Lower blood pressure.

- Less pain.

- Fewer colds.

- Enhanced sleep.

- Less likelihood of hypertension, diabetes, or a stroke.

- Longer, healthier lives.

MODULE 3

Foundational Concept IV

Game Theory: Clear Rules, Clear Consequences and Right Back in the Game of Greatness!

Think back to the tale *"Creative Recognitions, Inc."* and the response of Justice's leaders when they caught him texting his girlfriend while on the job. One ignored the behavior, although he clearly saw it. Another called him out on it, but relented when Justice assured him that it was just a quick message. And then, another member of Team Chrysalis gave him a full-on, sit-down-in-my-office lecture and threatened further disciplinary action. All three of these leaders saw the same infraction, but their reactions couldn't have been more different.

When leaders fail to strictly and clearly delineate and enforce rules they enable and allow rule breaking and the pushing of boundaries around rules. This is a surefire recipe for negativity as some employees dance around the rules to see how far they can push them. This isn't because employees are ill intentioned or bad people; it's just the natural pull of that uncertainty. They are leaking negative energy by rule breaking because they can or because they are not motivated to be in compliance. It's up to leadership to refuse to connect with them around negativity and to instead choose, consistently and firmly, to create connection around greatness.

The Nurtured Heart Approach®'s answer is to hold up video games (or pinball games for those of us who were born too early to have gotten on the video game bandwagon) as a model for effective rule making and enforcement. These games are designed to offer ***continuous positive reinforcement*** in the form of points, sounds, and visuals for as long as the player is successful. Research shows us one reason why these games are so compelling is that the continuous positive reinforcement of these games stimulate the area of the brain concerned with rewards and pleasure, making it enticing to play for hours on end. (Welsh, 2011) When a rule is broken or the player loses the game, the positive reinforcement stops...but all it takes to get back in the game is a simple reset, and the whole thing with all its pleasure starts all over again. No adverse consequences, no punishment, no penalty—just an unceremonious reset to get back in the game.

Think about your favorite sport. How are the rules enforced? In response to a foul, an immediate penalty is imposed, but then the game continues. In response to a broken rule or a lost point, the referees generally blow a whistle, call it what it is, then get the players right back in the game.

So, with this idea in mind, how might Team Chrysalis react to Justice's infraction in a way that would present a unified front and that would energize Justice to greatness instead of causing him to feel isolated, unmotivated, and ashamed? In the Nurtured Heart Approach®, the response to a broken rule is a simple, un-energized reset or timeout, just like those in the video games or sports and a warmhearted welcome back to success as soon as rule-breaking stops. This technique will be described in much greater detail later on.

So you see, game theory in the NHA is about *clearly* enforcing rules *without energizing* rule breaking, and about encouraging rule compliance by energizing that compliance while it is happening.

 KEYS TO SUCCESS

> **Choose to clearly define rules and to consistently refuse to energize the breaking of rules (or the pushing of boundaries around rules).**
>
> **When disciplinary action is necessary, give it in an un-energized fashion. All energized response comes when rules are not being broken.**
>
> **This, together with the intention to energize success, is the NHA's default setting. We energize success and refuse to energize negativity.**

MODULE 3

Worksheet #10: *"Be Self-Aware of Negativity Triggers"*

Date: _____

Write some examples of things that cause you to react with negativity. You know, those times when someone breaks a rule or does something to really make you want to lose your temper. Writing down your usual way of reacting will help you pinpoint areas where you need to practice enforcing rules without energizing rule breaking.

What Things Cause Me to React with Negativity?	How Do I React?	What Could I Do Differently?
Ex: When I catch an employee wasting time on personal emails.	Ex: I lecture them on company policy loudly enough to make sure that they are embarrassed and that as many people as possible can hear me.	Ex. I could randomly pop in on that employee and energize them for being engaged, working hard, and staying on target with our team goals.

WORKSHEET #10

Positivity Pulse Points

- From the first day a person experiences a new workplace, he or she begins at the earliest stages of development and socialization in the organization. They are being taught and are learning the unique culture. Bring them in and nourish them with all the emotional nutrients required for positive growth and change and they will flourish.

- Positive recognitions are energizing in a way which support and encourage the recipient to feel connected to the giver and to continue striving to develop and be their best self.

- Negativity saps energy but can also encourage the recipient to seek attention by making more negative choices.

- People can languish or just give their minimum effort at work when deprived of positive social, emotional, and intellectual relationships.

- To feel emotionally connected to others is a basic human need. The stronger the positive relationship connections one has, the more that person will flourish.

- Having a voice, feeling appreciated, valued, and connected are the real key factors that inspire team members to create happiness and greatness within an organization.

ACTION STEP 1: Identify one person at work who pushes your buttons and gets your attention with negative behavior. Resolve to take action at least once each day this week and say something positive to them *before* they have a chance to act out. To whom and what will you say?

_____

_____

_____

_____

ACTION STEP 2: Identify one person at work that needs guidance in doing a task. Remember Baby Steps and set the bar for them as low as possible so that you can acknowledge their success. For whom and how will you set the bar low to create success?

_____

_____

_____

_____

ACTION STEP 3: Identify at least one rule at work that often gets pushed to the limits. Notice and write down whether or not the rule is stated unclearly.

_____

_____

_____

_____

POSITIVITY
PULSE
FOR ORGANIZATIONS

Answer the following questions:

1. What did you set out to do by starting this module?

_____

_____

_____

2. What did you accomplish?

_____

_____

_____

3. What do you need to change to be the person you want to be?

_____

_____

_____

4. What is the Pearl of Positivity Wisdom you received this week?

_____

_____

_____

5. What is your Action Step *WOWEE* (Within One Week to Energize and Excel) intention you will commit to for this upcoming week?

_____

_____

_____

A S S E S S M E N T   M O D U L E   # **3**

IGNITE

People who are not clear about those guiding principles for which they truly stand can never expect to lay a foundation for trust and credibility, let alone develop the capacity to exercise leadership. Great leaders understand that every moment of everyday is a symbolic opportunity to communicate their values. They do not underestimate the power of personal example. Through their daily choices leaders carve out the character and reputation of the organization. In doing so they provide the standard by which others calibrate the appropriateness of their own behaviors.

~ Jackie and Kevin Freiberg

NOTES

IGNITE

MODULE 4

Support
Three Stands™ that Support the Methods

In Module 3 you discovered the four key concepts that are the foundation for building a Positivity Pulse in your relationships. Here in Module 4 you'll learn the Three Stands™ that support the method. You can think of them like a tripod, each supporting the other, together strong.

While you may be anxious to jump ahead to the next modules, it is important to build your understanding of the method because each layer is necessary for you to be able to successfully implement the approach so that it becomes your own "default method" of relating. These three stands—or commandments—provide clarity and are the underpinnings for the methods you will learn in the next two modules.

Module 4 Objectives

- To learn the Three Stands™ that will give you clear direction and resolve.

- To establish values and rules to live by.

Module 4 Summary

- Stand One: Refuse to leak negativity.

- Stand Two: Resolve to purposefully create and nurture success.

- Establishing workplace values makes compliance all about supporting the values.

- Stand Three: Resolve to have clear rules and clear, consistent consequences.

The Three Stands™: Clear-Cut Commandments

The Three Stands™ are the support system of this approach. Any time you aren't sure how to act or react to a situation, checking back in with the Three Stands™ will give you direction and resolve. (The recognition strategies described in the next sessions are the "how" to implement the approach, and all work to uphold these stands.)

STAND ONE

Refuse to leak negativity.

Not sure what a "negativity leak" might look like? It's happening any time:

- You lose your cool when a rule has been broken.

- Problems or issues captivate and elicit your charged response.

- You expect an employee to do something wrong so you can reprimand him.

- You are willing to focus energy and attention on poor choices.

- Employees are able to "push your buttons" by making poor choices or breaking rules.

When you have a "negativity leak" you give relationship in the form of recognition. Energy flows more strongly as a result of the employee doing something less than acceptable—leading the employee to perceive, on a deep, subconscious level, that more recognition and attention is available in response to wrong behavior.

 **KEYS TO SUCCESS**

Stand One is about not undermining the efficacy of the approach by "leaking" negativity. This said, it is important to realize that everybody leaks negative energy sometimes. Luckily, this approach does not require perfect execution in order to effect massive change. We're all human and we all make mistakes and leak negative energy at times. It's how we rebound from that mistake or leakage that makes the difference. As soon as you notice a leak, you can change course and step cleanly into a new moment of positivity.

WORKSHEET #11: Module 4

Worksheet #11: *"Places Where I Leak Negativity"*   Date: _____

Okay, it's time to "fess up." Even if you resolve to practice these stands as if your life depends on it, you're only human, and even you will leak at times. In order to help you become more aware of *where* or *when* or *with whom* you need to be on your best guard, be proactive and make a list right now. Give specific examples.

EXAMPLE: I tend to lose my temper or patience with _____

when they _____.

EXAMPLE: When the _____ rule is

broken, I tend to lecture on and on about _____.

1. _____
   _____

2. _____
   _____

3. _____
   _____

4. _____
   _____

5. _____
   _____

STAND TWO

Resolve to purposefully create and nurture success and greatness.

Relentlessly and strategically draw your team members into new and renewed patterns of success and greatness.

Think back to Baby Steps and the Toll Taker. We change our view and note what we are grateful for and we catch and create successful moments in our lives. And don't forget the Toll Taker with his positive message—you get to choose how you see things—whether you decide to see what's strong or what's wrong. The decision is up to you. Once that resolution is made, you can use the techniques for creating and energizing success and positivity that are covered in the next two sessions.

By *choosing to notice and energize* what's right, we show team members that their favorite toys "do lots of cool stuff" when they are successful, and that those toys get boring when rules are broken, boundaries are pushed, or they fail to show up as the great beings they are.

SUCCESS STORY

One of our clients is a lovely lady who had come to dread her job. She was head of Human Resources Department at her company and she thought her job was to find what was wrong with each employee and figure out how to fix them. As she is a caring and giving person at heart, this task was sapping her energy and making her sick.

She knew deep down inside that something was terribly wrong, and when she heard about our Positivity Pulse program, she jumped at the chance to figure out why she was not happy. To her great surprise and relief, she learned she could choose to see what was strong and good about each person, and work with them to nurture their success. She told us: "This program has changed my life! I realized I don't have to be the bad guy looking for everything wrong about each person. I can look for the positive and nurture them. I am so happy now. I love my job!"

Firmly Establish Your Values Before You Set the Rules

Oops! Maybe you're anxious to jump right in and learn how to enforce your organization's rules, but forgot to establish your values first. Do not move forward to set or enforce established rules until you establish your values first. This is because values have to be shared and understood *before* rules are created. Here's why: when everyone agrees that each chosen value represents strongly held and shared beliefs, they intuitively know why a corresponding rule is established. They are there to support the values. After everyone knows and agrees upon the values, then the rules make much more sense. "Here are the rules we agreed upon because we need to have ways to uphold our shared values." See how much easier it is to get compliance versus, "Here are the rules that you must follow because we say you must." Adherence to the values is what creates buy-in for the rules and drives decisions for the organization. Then, decisions will be based on upholding the values and disciplinary action stems from a disregard for those values.

What a positive difference shared values make—they help define the community and what is important to them as a group. So if you haven't yet defined your values, or they don't correspond to your rules, now is a great time to figure those out.

For example, if an organization has these stated values:

- We honor and respect one another and the people we serve.

- We treat everyone with dignity and respect.

- We care about each and every person with whom we are in contact and his or her safety is of the utmost importance.

Then three obvious rules that could come from these values would be:

- No passive-aggressive statements.

- No gossiping about one another.

- No teasing.

Below are some other examples of one organization's values:

- With peace, perseverance, and hard work we will not fail to reach our goals.

- We communicate openly and move toward harmonious solutions.

- We are aware that oppression exists and believe in equal treatment regardless of race, gender, sexual orientation, religion, age, or cultural ethnicity. Everyone's voice holds value.

- We are committed to high level quality care and work to improve our system's performance through continued learning, research, and development.

- We uphold ethical standards both in business and clinical practice.

- We realize that people do not care about how much we know but rather how much we care.

- We acknowledge that consistency and commitment to service provision is key to creating success.

When the values are shared and understood it makes for a much more peaceful way of reviewing the rules in any environment. And when recognitions noticing values are sincerely given they serve to accelerate employees' compliance and spiral positivity.

"The servant leader feels that once the direction is clear, his or her role is to help people achieve their goals. The servant leader seeks to help people win through teaching and coaching individuals so that they can do their best. You need to listen to your people, praise them, support them and redirect them when they deviate from their goals."

~ Ken Blanchard, The Servant Leader

Character Strengths, Values, and Virtues

In their book *Character Strengths and Virtues* the late Christopher Peterson and positive psychology pioneer Martin Seligman expand on the notions of character, values, and virtues by creating and defining six categories of human strengths that are valued across cultures:

- Strengths of wisdom and knowledge—creativity, curiosity, open-mindedness, love of learning, perspective.

- Strengths of courage—bravery, persistence, integrity, vitality.

- Strengths of humanity—love, kindness, social intelligence.

- Strengths of justice—citizenship, fairness, leadership.

- Strengths of temperance—forgiveness, mercy, humility, modesty, prudence, self-regulation (self-control).

- Strengths of transcendence—appreciation of beauty and excellence, gratitude, hope, humor, spirituality. (Peterson and Seligman, 2004)

Consider how the values that are important to you might fall into these categories. On any given day, you can choose which category you would like most to acknowledge in your workplace.

Worksheet #12: Team Worksheet—*"Our Values"*   Date: _____

Are any of the above categories of character strengths and virtues explicitly valued in your workplace? Are there written values already stated? If so, list them below. If not, which ones do you feel could be important to your employees to strive for to serve each other and your customers, and to further the mission of your company?

List the values individually or group into categories.

_____

_____

_____

_____

_____

_____

_____

With the notes you made above, decide upon or state your company values in phrases or sentences so that all may know them.

_____

_____

_____

_____

_____

_____

_____

Worksheet #13: *"Celebrate Success"*   Date: _____

One terrific way to nurture success is to have ways to energize and celebrate employees for success when they least expect it. A little extra effort on your part goes a long way to make them feel seen, valued, and appreciated. Brainstorm and list some ways that you could celebrate them in a meaningful manner that might surprise them. For example you could send them a nice email or leave them a personal recognition on a brightly colored Post–It® note.

1. _____

    _____

2. _____

    _____

3. _____

    _____

4. _____

    _____

5. _____

    _____

WORKSHEET #13

STAND THREE

Resolve to have clear rules and clean, consistent, and effective consequences when those rules are broken.

This stand is about knowing the rules and policies cold, about reinforcing and encouraging team members for not breaking them, and about being absolutely consistent about giving a consequence whenever rules are broken. When a rule is being broken, reset the employee back to greatness, welcome him or her back "into the game" and move right on to the next moment of success. Don't give energy to the problem of a broken rule—on the contrary, problems get no emotional play. No backlash, no long-term repercussions. Just a reset and then an openhearted invitation back to the greatness that was always there.

A Word About Using Resets

By now you might be wondering how you can enforce the rules. You start by withdrawing energetic connection. Enforce a broken rule with as little energy, emotion, and drama as possible. Remember when Mrs. Crabtree engaged Justice with a long lecture. She demonstrated to him that her energy was most accessible in response to the breaking of a rule. It might not have been pleasant for Justice, but it gave him something he felt he needed: an intense connection with someone on the leadership team. Unfortunately, he hadn't been able to find a way to connect by following the rules. He didn't get connection when he was following the rules, only when he was breaking them.

To avoid this dynamic, refuse to give your precious energy to problems. In Module 6, you will learn about using a "reset" as an immediate consequence of breaking a rule. You will learn to take a stand (as in Stand Three) to enforce the rules.

BUT FIRST - you need to learn the energizing methods in the next two chapters. Before you start using resets it's VERY IMPORTANT to deepen your relationships with the positive recognitions you will be learning in the next two modules to begin to shift any negative dynamics. Then when a rule is broken, just reset the rule-breaker and find a way to welcome him or her into the next success.

State Rules in the Negative

Begin to manifest Stand Three by stating rules in the negative. This makes "in-bounds" and "out-of-bounds" absolutely clear. Remember the Game Theory concept. If the rules are *not* stated in the negative, then where is the line of non-compliance? By not having them stated in the negative, there is too much room for pushing the limits. With clarity comes better understanding for all. For example:

- NO personal cell phone use.

- NO coming in late.

- NO negative attitude.

- NO sarcastic comments.

- NO racist, sexist, homophobic, ageist, or religious jokes or comments.

- NO unprofessional attire.

WORKSHEET #14: Module 4

Worksheet #14: Team Worksheet—*"Our Rules"*   Date: _____

If your organization does NOT already have written rules, it's time to write them.

If you already have written rules stated in the negative, go on to the next exercise.

Looking back to the Team Worksheet: "Our Values," write rules in the negative that correspond to your stated values.

For example, the values statement: We uphold ethical standards both in business and clinical practice.

The rule: No unethical behaviors.

_____

_____

_____

_____

_____

_____

_____

_____

_____

_____

_____

_____

_____

_____

The 7 Steps To Ignite Flourishing In Leaders, Teams And Organizations

Positivity Pulse Points

- Refuse to give energy to negativity.

- Resolve to energize success no matter what—even if you think the employee is just doing what they are supposed to do.

- Shared values are important to creating shared culture. From the values, rules will logically follow.

- Resolve to have clear rules, stated in the negative where possible.

- Adhere to the Three Stands™ with unwavering conviction and the energy in your workplace will quickly shift.

ACTION STEP 1: Resolve to nurture success this week. Spread your positive comments around to several co-workers. Each day, say at least one positive comment more than you would ordinarily say to each of them. Jot down to whom, what you said, and their reaction.

_____

_____

_____

ACTION STEP 2: Is there a particular person you seem to have the most negative interactions with at work? Notice the circumstances that seem to initiate negativity. Use the concepts you are learning to try and decipher if the person is looking for more connection with you. Write what you notice.

_____

_____

_____

ACTION STEP 3: Be mindful of your own thoughts as you go through each day. When does negative self-talk come up in you? (If none—congratulations!)

_____

_____

_____

POSITIVITY
PULSE
FOR **ORGANIZATIONS**

Answer the following questions:

1. **What did you set out to do by starting this module?**

_____

_____

_____

2. **What did you accomplish?**

_____

_____

_____

3. **What do you need to change to be the person you want to be?**

_____

_____

_____

4. **What is the Pearl of Positivity Wisdom you received this week?**

_____

_____

_____

5. **What is your Action Step _WOWEE_ (Within One Week to Energize and Excel) intention you will commit to for this upcoming week?**

_____

_____

_____

ASSESSMENT MODULE #

4

IGNITE

"Learning to get a Positivity Pulse is like learning a new language, and like any new language, it takes practice and perseverance. It demands that we stop leaking our own negativity while holding a mindset that is governed by open-mindedness and open-heartedness."

~ Sherry Blair

NOTES

IGNITE

MODULE 5

Discover
Strategies to Support the Stands

Your awareness of communication habits has been opened, you understand the Foundational Concepts, and you have learned the Three Stands™ that support the methods of growing positivity and flourishing in your workplace. In this module, you will learn the first two recognitions that help you create an upward spiral of positivity.

Apply these strategies daily, like your life depends on it. Sprinkle them around on everyone you come into contact with and you'll beam heart energy all day long—and so will those you recognize!

Module 5 Objectives

- To discover what Active Recognitions are and how to use them to make others feel seen, valued, and appreciated.

- To discover what Experiential Recognitions are and how to use them to reinforce and increase "Inner Wealth™."

- To become more aware of greatness happening all around you and how to celebrate it.

- To learn how to address negativity and noncompliance and reset back to greatness.

MODULE 5

Module 5 Summary

- Active Recognitions: a verbal snapshot of what an employee is doing when he or she is acting positively.

- Experiential Recognitions: expanding on an Active Recognition by adding a description of values being reflected in an employee's positive choices, behaviors, and decisions.

- Values and character strengths can be appreciated, amplified, and strengthened by using recognitions.

- Resets are used to redirect self and others from negativity back to positivity.

Strategy 1: Active Recognitions*

Active Recognitions are so simple to do that at first you might feel they are insignificant. But don't be fooled! They are so profound that they can notch up the positive energy between two people or even throughout the workplace very quickly.

An Active Recognition is simply giving a verbal snapshot of what you see when a person is acting positively. You are not giving any kind of judgment. For example, "Jonathan, I notice you're at work early today."

How to Give an Active Recognition:

- **Step 1. Clearly observe what the employee is doing when he or she is acting in a positive manner.**

- **Step 2. Offer a "verbal snapshot" of what you see, avoiding any kind of judgment.**

- **The most useful words for giving Active Recognitions are "I notice" and "I see."**

- **Stay in the here and now.**

- **Do NOT lecture, preach, or leak negative energy about how "it's better than last time…"**

- **Use this technique throughout the day for each employee, as often as you can.**

Example: "Joe, I notice your desktop and files are so neatly organized."

MODULE 5

Even if the employee is just doing what they are supposed to be doing, consider all the ways in which he's being successful and making choices that are positive. Most of us aren't accustomed to acknowledging others for the little things they do *right*. As one manager asked, "Why should I acknowledge anyone for doing what they are paid to do?" The reason why is that you want to *change* the energy of the individual relationships and the culture at large. You want to notch up the Positivity Pulse in your organization—and it starts with *you* giving positive energy to everyone you can, one person at a time. In no time at all, you will notice employees starting to give recognitions to others, and so the positivity spirals upward!

"Michael, I heard that your client was really challenging, and you stayed calm."

"Julie, you are doing great at multitasking today! Thanks for asking for that checklist to help you stay organized."

"Naveen, I see you've brought food from home for lunch today. It has such a rich aroma and looks incredibly healthy."

"Drew, I notice how caring you are about your co-workers."

"Sarwat, that's such a colorful head scarf. It really brightens up the room!"

"ToniAnne, it's clear to me you are so excited to learn new things."

"Shana, I notice you brighten the whole office with your big smiles and positive energy."

* Originally, Active Recognitions were referred to as Kodak Moments. Imagine it as if you are taking a picture and simply stating exactly what you see.

 **KEYS TO SUCCESS**

By relaying the picture exactly as we see it and calling out the positive attributes being demonstrated, the person feels seen, acknowledged, and appreciated.

Use Active Recognitions:

- Only for positive moments (remember the Toll Taker: that if you choose, you can see positivity almost anywhere). Be aware that positive moments are also those moments when we are handling ourselves with grace and dignity and respect toward others even when we are angry or frustrated.

- Never in reference to rule-breaking or negative behavior.

- By employing neutral, non-judgmental language to make the message as "digestible" as possible.

- With as much specificity and details as possible.

With these simple recognitions you are laying the foundation that will allow you to take the approach deeper with added texture and more heart-felt compassion as you move into using the next three techniques, all of which build on the first one. With each recognition, you are helping that person feel seen in a new way. Repeated recognitions, especially as you go deeper with the approach, build what we call Inner Wealth™, which means the person starts to "own" those positive qualities you are calling to their attention.

WORKSHEET #15: Module 5

POSITIVITY PULSE FOR **ORGANIZATIONS**

Worksheet #15: *"Using Active Recognitions"*   Date: _____

Reference the guide below, and then write your own examples.

Use Active Recognitions to:

- State that you value an employee for who he or she is in that moment.

- Prove that no one is "invisible."

- See and celebrate each employee.

- Open conversations that can lead to respectful cultural awareness.

- Enhance positive regard and conversations around diversity.

EXAMPLE: "Camille, you are so wonderful at reorganizing our office after our big move."

1. _____

   _____

2. _____

   _____

3. _____

   _____

4. _____

   _____

5. _____

   _____

Worksheet #16: *"Practicing Active Recognitions"*   Date: _____

It feels great to be the recipient of positive recognitions. It also feels great to give them. If at first you feel awkward, GREAT! That just means you are stretching a little and learning a new way of relating. It will become easier and easier—and pretty soon it will become automatic!

Using this table to help you break down the different stages of interaction will make you aware of both sides of the interaction—the POSITIVITY PULSE.

ASSIGNMENT: At least three times in the morning and three times in the afternoon, give an Active Recognition and note it on the table below. This includes virtual recognizing in emails, texts, instant messages, instagrams, etc.

HINT: Print out pages to keep handy for use each day this week.

* **Extra points for practicing and noting more than six times per day!**

What You Saw or Noticed	What You Said	Recipient's Response	How You Felt

MODULE 5

Strategy 2: Experiential Recognitions

With this technique, you build on Active Recognitions by adding a description of values being reflected in the employee's positive choices. With this strategy, capture the employee in the moment of living desirable values and demonstrating strengths. In this way, you continue to build Inner Wealth™ and reinforce character strengths, values, and virtues.

When you use this type of recognition, you are amplifying Active Recognitions by including a positive judgment and/or value attached to the statement. Give recognitions and appreciations that are specific, detailed, and based on observable positive behavior.

Positive values are behaviors or thoughts deemed by society as intrinsically good or worthy of imitating. A list of values and strengths you might want to acknowledge and strengthen in your workplace might include:

Adaptability	Good sportsmanship	Peaceful
Altruism	Hardworking	Professionalism
Being a positive role model	Helpfulness	Resolve
	Honesty	Resourceful
Caring	Humility	Respect
Compassion	Inner strength	Responsibility
Commitment	Integrity	Self-control
Confidence	Inventive	Self-motivated
Cooperation	Kindness	Team player
Courage	Leadership	Thoughtfulness
Creativity	Loyalty	Tolerance
Cultural sensitivity	Motivated to grow and learn	Using good judgment
Determination		Using good manners
Enthusiasm	Open-heartedness	Wisdom
Expressiveness	Open-mindedness	
Fairness	Patience	

TYSON'S STORY

One night after working late, I noticed two of our staff from the facilities department tending to their responsibilities. They both seemed to be working so hard and it was rather late at night. I stopped to thank them for taking such good care of our building and told them I appreciated how hard they were working. They seemed surprised that I even took the time out to acknowledge them, never mind commend them on a job well done. I thought to myself, these folks could have been my parents, working these shifts to support our family, and I would hope that someone was kind and considerate toward them.

Tyson Toles, Senior Counsel

Global Projects Operation

GE Power and Water

Schenectady, NY

How to Give an Experiential Recognition:

- **Step 1. Start with an Active Recognition (Clearly observe what the employee is doing when he or she is acting in a positive manner).**

- **Step 2. Add a comment that reflects a value or strength.**

- **Apply this technique when a team member is doing a great job and/or is following the rules.**

- **Be genuine and show excitement (in your own way).**

- **Remember Baby Steps and the Toll Taker.**

- **Use this technique throughout the day for each employee, as often as you can.**

Example: "Joe, I notice your desktop and files are so neatly organized. What a positive role model you are!"

Remember Mrs. Polaroid, who flows gracefully in her ability to experientially recognize the people with whom she comes into contact daily? As a more seasoned manager, she has the ability to use positive judgments and value statements to develop and deepen characteristic strengths and virtues. She does it in her own unique, intense style—and you can too.

Experiential Recognition is a right-in-the-moment opportunity to anchor employees in the values, philosophy, policies, and procedures of the workplace. This is how to move beyond the "thank you" or "great job" we have been using conventionally. Here you have the golden opportunity to further enforce a company's philosophy, vision, and mission statement as well as rules and regulations on a daily basis.

"Michael, I heard that your client was really challenging, and you stayed calm and handled it with true professionalism."*

"Julie, you are doing great at multitasking today! Thanks for asking for that checklist to help you stay organized. This shows your willingness to want to do your job even better."*

"Drew, I notice how caring you are about your co-workers. This shows your compassion and your commitment to a positive workplace."*

"ToniAnne, it's clear to me you are so excited to learn new things. This shows me you are motivated to grow and learn."*

"Travis, I see how hard you are working to meet our short deadline. You show such a strong work commitment to our project. What a strong work ethic you have!"*

*Originally, Experiential Recognitions were referred to as Polaroids.

 KEYS TO SUCCESS

- **Focus on recognizing qualities and strengths you want to see grow.**

- **Give recognitions early and often—daily! Walk the halls or just pop in on employees.**

- **Don't be discouraged if you are met with resistance. Remember Stand Two: Resolve to purposefully create and nurture success and greatness. Be relentless.**

"In time, feeling ownership of a myriad of positive qualities leads to more confidence."

~ Sherry Blair

Worksheet #17: Team Worksheet—*"Top Character Strengths of My Team"*

Date: _____

A. Gather your team members who are also using this program. Based on your experience with your team, take a few minutes, (seven or so) and list the top three character strengths you feel you and each of two other team members exhibit. Give a short example of how/when those strengths are evident. (Don't forget to list yourself as one of the three.)

Team Member _____

1. _____

2. _____

3. _____

Team Member _____

1. _____

2. _____

3. _____

Team Member _____

1. _____

2. _____

3. _____

B. Next, take turns comparing your list to the strengths each reported and discuss which ones you noted and why. Notice if you chose the same or similar strengths for the same people.

C. Use your new tool of Experiential Recognition to write an Experiential Recognition for each strength you listed. Then have fun taking turns recognizing each of them out loud.

Team Member _____

1. _____

2. _____

3. _____

Team Member _____

1. _____

2. _____

3. _____

Team Member _____

1. _____

2. _____

3. _____

The Nurtured Heart Approach® is not a "soft" approach. It's about purposefully and relentlessly creating, nurturing, and celebrating success and greatness. It's about knowing the rules cold and reinforcing and encouraging team members for not breaking them, and being absolutely consistent about giving a reset consequence whenever rules are broken. The techniques you will learn in this and the next module will have you igniting greatness wherever you go.

WORKSHEET #

Positivity Pulse Points

- When even small details are positively noticed and recognized out loud (or through written communication), the recipient feels irrefutably noticed, acknowledged, and appreciated for *doing what she is supposed to be doing*—working, following rules, and showing positivity.

- As soon as a new employee starts work, recognitions can be used to begin to teach him or her about the Positivity Pulse culture you are nurturing.

- Using recognitions instead of the usual perfunctory salutations proves to employees that they are not invisible—they are "seen" and celebrated each time they walk through the door.

- No matter what the position, everyone in the workplace has a right to be acknowledged and treated with dignity, respect, and integrity. In this very moment, they are participating in making that workplace run like a finely tuned engine. Everyone deserves proper emotional nourishment and feedback for contributions to the Positivity Pulse in your organization. Every employee deserves to be energetically nourished for his or her role in the workplace.

- By using Active and Experiential Recognitions, you are seeing, naming, and appreciating the greatness you see in people all around you.

- Notice diversity in the workplace and use recognitions to encourage conversations for deeper appreciation and understanding of cultural differences.

ACTION STEP 1: Choose one co-worker to be your "Recognition Buddy." Resolve to recognize each other with Active and/or Experiential Recognitions at least 10 times each day. (Even if you were to say several sentences for 15 seconds for each recognition that is only a total of two and a half minutes!) This approach doesn't take much of your time throughout the day. Really. Just become aware of what people are doing and energize them with a few sentences at a time. If you practice daily, it will become a habit! List some ideas to get you started:

_____

_____

_____

ACTION STEP 2: Make your own list of qualities, strengths, and values you admire. Copy them on a paper or put them in your calendar or other electronic device so you can keep them handy, and each day choose one to focus on. Actively seek evidence of it in a co-worker, and then recognize them.

_____

_____

_____

ACTION STEP 3: Find employees that you do not ordinarily interact with on a daily basis, especially those that might be the gatekeepers of your organization, like receptionists, security staff and those who maintain the grounds and facilities. Make it your habit to recognize and appreciate them daily. List some people and things they do to get you started:

_____

_____

_____

ASSESSMENT: Module 5

Answer the following questions:

1. **What did you set out to do by starting this module?**

   _____

   _____

   _____

2. **What did you accomplish?**

   _____

   _____

   _____

3. **What do you need to change to be the person you want to be?**

   _____

   _____

   _____

4. ⬤ **What is the Pearl of Positivity Wisdom you received this week?**

   _____

   _____

   _____

5. **What is your Action Step _WOWEE_ (Within One Week to Energize and Excel) intention you will commit to for this upcoming week?**

   _____

   _____

   _____

"Remember, your most valuable resources drive away at the end of every business day, and it is your job to make sure they are eager to return the next morning."

~ Kevin and Jackie Frieberg,
American authors

NOTES

IGNITE

MODULE 6

Accelerate
Strategies to Spiral Positivity

You already have tools to consistently recognize and notice positivity flourishing all around you. With daily practice you will cultivate even more positive energy for yourself and others.

In this module, you'll learn how to creatively promote compliance with your organization's policies and procedures, and how to create successes that would not otherwise exist.

You'll also learn how to deal with difficult and/or underachieving employees, and how to reset them back to greatness.

Module 6 Objectives

- To discover what Proactive Recognitions are and how to accelerate employees' compliance with your organization's rules, procedures, and policies.

- To learn what Creative Recognitions are and how to confidently use them to create abundant success and positivity for every employee.

- To discover that giving "resets" can accelerate positivity for yourself as well as others.

Module 6 Summary

- By focusing on and appreciating positive accomplishments instead of dwelling on what is not done, you energize the team member's desire to achieve greatness.

- When a manager, frontline worker, or other employee's well-being is supported, he or

she can thrive creatively, intellectually, emotionally, and socially, and this comes back to benefit everyone in the workplace.

- A "reset" can be any word or signal you choose, as long as it holds the idea of pausing during a moment of rule-breaking and creating an opportunity to jump into a new moment of greatness. Sometimes a moment of silence can reset yourself and everyone back to a calm, peaceful state of being.

Strategy 3: Proactive Recognitions*

Proactive Recognitions build on both Active and Experiential Recognitions, but with an important twist: we notice and verbally acknowledge moments where an employee is not breaking rules.

What?! This might sound absurd at first but ultimately this technique can be incredibly energizing! Intentional celebrations of moments where problems are not occurring give you vast opportunities for positive reflections. Rather than giving energy to a person only when a rule is being broken or there's a threat of it being broken, this technique gives energy in response to rules not broken. The employee comes to see that much positive attention is available in return for remaining in compliance with the organization's policies and procedures. Giving a Proactive Recognition is much easier than it may sound. Read on to learn how and you'll be a pro before long!

Establish Values First Before Rules

Let's review the Values to Rules Positivity Pulse concept from Module 4. Be sure you established and have a very clear understanding of what the values are in your organization. Values have to be understood before rules are created. When everyone understands each value, they intuitively know what the negatively stated rule is that upholds the value. Adherence to the values is what creates buy-in for the rules and drives decisions for the organization. Decisions are based on upholding the values and disciplinary action stems from a disregard for those values.

For example, if an organization has these stated values:

- We are committed to creating a peaceful and healthy environment in which to work.

- We honor and respect one another and the people we serve.

- We treat everyone with dignity and respect.

- We care about each and every person with whom we are in contact and his or her safety is of the utmost importance.

Then two obvious rules that could come from these values would be:

- No gossiping.

- No smoking except in designated areas.

When the values are shared and understood it makes for such a more peaceful way of reviewing the rules in any environment. And when Proactive Recognitions are sincerely given they serve to accelerate employees' compliance and spiral positivity.

State Rules in the Negative

Proactive Recognitions begin with leaders in the workplace who understand and live by the values—that's you. If you didn't review or write your rules in Module 4, go back and work through Module 4. Do it now. Take a deep dive into your policy and procedures manual and start getting a complete grasp of your workplace's rules and policies. Then make sure the rules stem naturally from your organization's values and are stated precisely and negatively (starting with the word "No..."). Rules or policies may require modification to fit these parameters. If this is the case, then get to it!

Once those rules and policies have been established or re-established, they need to be clearly and strictly upheld. Here are several examples of workplace rules:

- No personal cell phone use while working.

- No coming late to work or back from breaks.

- No smoking in front of the building.

- No gossiping about one another.

- No cross-talking in meetings.

- No passive-aggressive statements.

- No personal use of the Internet while at work.

- No teasing.

Proactive Recognitions inspire employees to comply with rules, regulations, and policies without creating adversarial relationships. They accelerate and deepen the refusal to energize negativity, moving the employee into a new realm of success and counteracting the tendency to create energized relationship around noncompliance. It's a great way to tap into heart-centered proactivity and to gently reset away from negative reactivity.

Let's Take a Look at Proactive Recognition in Action!

❤ "Rajinder, I heard your personal cell phone ringing and noticed you didn't answer it, but instead quickly put it in silent mode. Thank you for following our policy about personal cell phone use in the workplace!"

❤ "Michael, I know you got frustrated with that co-worker who did not do her job, but you remained calm. You didn't curse and you were helpful. By staying in control, you're helping us maintain a positive and peaceful environment."

❤ "Marcelo, I see that you are showing up several minutes before your shift starts. I appreciate your efforts to be ready to start on time! It helps us all start the shift off on a great note when everyone is supporting our on-time policy and ready to jump into action!"

Reflect on Baby Steps and the Toll Taker. Choose to see the rules that are followed and drop the rope as low as necessary to create success. Move away from reacting to rule breaking and into Proactive Recognition of rules and procedures followed.

*Originally, Proactive Recognitions were referred to as Canons.

How to Give a Proactive Recognition:

- Define workplace policies and procedures as negative rules that start with the word "No."

- Be on the lookout for the values being upheld and the rules followed, and make a point of recognizing employees for following the rules and upholding the associated value—especially for those who have a tendency to break particular rules repeatedly.

- Talk about policies and procedures in the context of their being followed rather than only bringing them up when someone isn't following them.

- Respond to broken rules, policies, or procedures with a reset—whether it's for someone else or for yourself.

- Move right back to greatness by recognizing the next success.

The Challenging Employee and the Underachieving Employee Explained

Although adults would seem to be too mature to act out to get attention in the ways a child would do, this isn't always the case. In the workplace, adult team members may fall into the same childish patterns. Some adults even seem to thrive on negative attention and all the drama that surrounds it.

Often co-workers and managers are baffled and challenged when dealing with this difficult type of employee. Such an employee is generally aware that repeated noncompliance may result in the loss of his or her job, but the need for energetic connection trumps this concern. If it's the only way to be energetically fed, he or she will go that route—although the quality of that nutrition is subpar and leaves the employee with a continuing feeling of lack and longing. When this type of employee is placed into a chaotic, unstructured environment where rules are blurry and management is inconsistent, negative energy leaks are exacerbated, and this employee becomes the energy leak in the system of the workplace.

Refuse to be sucked into creating energized relationships around problems, doubts, and worries. Instead, set your intention to create a positive workplace where people want to participate and have positive, productive relationships. When employees have challenges, shift the energy by finding a way to create success in that moment.

Then there are the extremely compliant employees who come to work every day on time, return from breaks punctually, complete all their tasks, and generally do not get involved in workplace banter or gossip. While they are good employees, they are not great employees because their workplace relationships do not inspire them. Because they're such good employees they get almost no attention in the workplace. They don't make waves. These accommodating employees may think their ideas do not matter because they have not been encouraged to come forth with those ideas. Don't take your good employees for granted. Do you appreciate how challenging

their workdays can be? Do you acknowledge them when they go above and beyond to hunt someone down in the face of an emergency or when they politely handle an irate customer? Don't let them go home each day feeling unseen, unsung, and unappreciated—or one day they just might not return—ever.

Your frontline workers are a source of hugely untapped potential. They are the very first people seen in the morning by the rest of your employees and your customers, and as such they are the gateway to positivity. They have the power to set the tone and mood for each day. Make sure to recognize and energize them on your way into the office and you will be helping to role model positivity and set a positive tone for the day.

The Magic of Transformation

Some difficult employees will not believe *your* new behavior is real or sustainable. They might test you with bouts of rule breaking practically in your face, trying to elicit your "normal" reactions of energizing their negativity. This is when you must be *determined* and *relentless* in practicing your new strategies. You must go to work and use all your new recognition tools to shower them with positive energy and refuse to energize their negativity. You have to show them you *have changed* and that you are sticking with it. Your sincerity and relentlessness in practicing your new strategies will eventually create a safe place for them to be able to accept this new positive attention and help them relax into *wanting* to be successful and being able to receive your positive attention. If you can really "see" the employee you might come to understand this may be the first time that someone important in their life really "sees" them, believes they can be successful, and holds a mirror for them to see proof that they are being successful. This unfolding transformation is the magic these methods hold.

Change Starts with Awareness of Our Habits

As a leader, you need to explore the ways in which negative behavior is enabled in your workplace. Has a blind eye been cast on the problem? Has there been silence about a particular rule until it has been broken so many times that someone explodes with negative energy in reaction to it? Does the rule-breaker get special treatment and one-on-one attention behind closed doors? Is there a second manager brought in to be the disciplinarian?

To root out negativity and rule breaking, each leader needs to be aware of their own habits. This next exercise will help you.

Worksheet #18: *"What's Your Disciplinary Style?"*   Date: _____

Take a moment to think about how you have been dealing with rule-breakers in your workplace. Do you treat them all the same? Or do some seem to pull for different treatment? List below how you normally deal with rule-breakers:

Infraction	How I deal with It
Example: Chronically missing deadlines	Example: Drag them into my office, next time give a written warning, then threaten a bad performance review

Everyone will be looking to you to see if you really are buying into this new approach with your consistency. Be relentless. Be determined. Practice using your new tools and challenge yourself to become skillful. As their role model, you set the expectations and the standards.

Using Resets

By now you might be wondering **how** you can enforce the rules. You start by withdrawing energetic connection. Enforce a broken rule with as little energy, emotion, and drama as possible. Remember when Mrs. Crabtree engaged Justice with a long lecture, she demonstrated to him that her energy was most accessible in response to the breaking of a rule. It might not have been pleasant for Justice, but it gave him something he felt he needed: an intense connection with someone on the leadership team. Unfortunately, he hadn't been able to find a way to connect by **following** the rules. He didn't get connection when he was following the rules, only when he was **breaking** them. Some adults, like some children, become very addicted to negative attention seeking behaviors.

To avoid this dynamic, refuse to give your precious energy to problems. In this approach, we use a "reset" as an immediate consequence of breaking a rule. A reset is about **taking a stand** (as in Stand Three) to enforce the rules.

Reset

What if a rule is not being followed? Using the word "reset" gives us an opportunity to remind ourselves and our staff that we can reset away from negativity as soon as we realize it is happening. Think of it as a keyword that supports us in ridding ourselves of a negative cognition, negative behavior, or an unhealthy negative emotion that arises as a knee-jerk reaction to that negativity.

That being said, "reset" isn't the only word that you can use. You can select a different word that works for your organization. Some simply raise one hand silently as a way to convey they are not energizing negativity—not even enough to speak about it or listen to it. Have some fun and find a way that fits with your culture. Even if it means running around the workplace blowing referee whistles, or holding a "reset" paddle aloft in a meeting. "Recalculate" is a word that can remind us of our inner GPS—the part of us that knows how to calmly recalculate when we make a wrong turn and guides us back in the right direction. "Reboot" is a meaningful word techies understand and might like to use. There are other fun ways by using humor if that works for you, but by no means do you use sarcasm.

It doesn't matter which word you decide on as long as everyone understands what it means. Let's say you overhear two employees gossiping. As you walk by you unceremoniously say, "Let's reset and get back to work." They should know full well why they were reset. But if you see a gaze of confusion about why the reset happened you can clear it up as soon as the gossiping

stops by giving a Proactive Recognition about the "NO gossiping" rule being followed and by acknowledging the value that is being upheld.

For example: You overhear Maddy and Carolyn gossiping about another employee when you are walking by. You unceremoniously say, "Maddy and Carolyn, reset yourselves now." By Maddy's quizzical gaze you realize she either doesn't understand why you reset her or is incredulous that you did. Either way, don't leak negativity by stopping to lecture her about the "No gossiping" policy. Instead, since she has quit speaking and is just staring at you, give her/them a Proactive Recognition. Say, "Thank you both for resetting so quickly. I appreciate your effort in helping all team members feel respected and knowing there is no gossiping allowed."

KEYS TO SUCCESS

Whichever word you decide on, if a rule is not being followed and the value is not being upheld it is time to give a simple, un-energized reset. Here's how it works. Let's say you see someone playing an online game. Simply state, "Let's reset and get back to work." or just "Reset."

No lectures, no warnings, no explanations.

Please note: This does not mean that a consequence for playing video games while at work would not be imposed. You just handle it unceremoniously with as little energy as possible. Admittedly, reset can be complex to understand and implement. More training, practice and coaching can be beneficial to help you through the learning curve.

Worksheet #19: *"Practice Resetting Yourself"*　　　Date: _____

One of the most powerful uses of the reset is in *resetting your own thoughts or negative behavior* away from negativity. Practice resetting yourself before you put some negative thoughts into words or a sarcastic email. Being a role model for this practice is key to making this transformation.

Let your co-workers know you're just as prepared to reset yourself as you are to reset them. Say it out loud: "Oops! Time to reset myself!" And then take yourself and your staff right back to the beat of the Positivity Pulse. Whatever the case, list a few examples below and commit to resetting yourself when you catch negativity brewing.

Example: When I wander off topic in a meeting and waste everyone's time.	Reset: I'm going to reset myself and get back on track in order for us to complete our agenda.

Strategy 4: Creative Recognition

Create Successes that Would Not Otherwise Exist

Creative Recognition builds on Active Recognition, using clear, simple commands and bigger-than-ordinary positive acknowledgements in response to even small gradations of compliance.

Think of Baby Steps and recognizing the slightest movement toward success. We celebrate short-term wins with our eye on long-term goal achievement.

Creative Recognition is a way of making those steps available and rewarding for even the most challenging employee. This strategy makes success unavoidable—and retrains the employee to trust that he'll get plenty of energized positive connections even in response to the smallest success.

For example:

- Valerie arrives on time to the office and heads in the direction of her desk. (You have noticed she has recently begun a habit of stopping by several other employees' desks and distracting them for quite a while before she actually starts work at her desk.) Applying your new strategy, as she is heading in the right direction you might say, "Valerie, I need you to go right to your desk and get started. It's going to be a busy day." As soon as she sits down, give her abundant recognition, "I see you're jumping right in. I so appreciate your energy and commitment."

- Another employee, Jordan, has a bad habit of interrupting people at meetings with ideas often completely off-topic. At the next meeting, you see him about to burst with something to say. You say, "Jordan, I see you are just about to burst with something to contribute, and I need you to wait until I get through this slide." He does. Then, ask for his input while giving recognitions, "I could see how frustrating it was for you to wait to volunteer your take on this issue. You demonstrated great patience even when I asked you to wait a little longer. Thanks for contributing so much to the respectful atmosphere of this meeting."

You can also creatively recognize employees for putting forth genuine effort, making difficult changes, overcoming obstacles, and staying on a trajectory of personal growth and ever-increasing achievement.

How to Give a Creative Recognition:

- Watch for clues suggesting that employees are about to do exactly what they are supposed to do, then make a request with which they're already on their way to complying. Voila! You've created a moment of success.

- When requests are complied with, give plentiful acknowledgment in the form of Experiential Recognition: what values or qualities is the employee upholding in his or her choices to comply with requests? Point out greatness qualities, character strengths, and virtues.

- For example: "Gloria, I know it has been hard for you to speak up and reset your employees that are breaking the "No personal cell phone at work policy." You are really taking control of the situation and stepping up as an effective manager. You're facing your biggest challenge in being assertive with your supervisees to stay on task and comply with our policies, and that shows me you are acting with courage and that your confidence is growing."

At times, due to time constraints, lack of funding, budget cuts, stress, emergencies, and the like, it's easy to get caught up in what is **not** done versus what is already accomplished or is being accomplished in that moment. By focusing on and appreciating positive accomplishments instead of worrying about or dwelling on what isn't done, you energize that team member's desire to achieve. When individual employees' spirits are supported by positive recognitions, he or she will flourish creatively, intellectually, emotionally, and socially, and this comes back to benefit everyone in the workplace, as well as impacting the bottom line for the better.

Creative Recognitions give leaders even more control over the flow of energy in the workplace. Employees get the sense there is a cultural shift underway, and that the old paradigm of energy for negativity is being replaced with a positive flow of energy. Guide your employees to make ever more successful choices that support their growth as well as the mission of your team and everyone benefits.

The Nurtured Heart® Warriors team at Creative Recognitions, Inc., understood this well. They knew intuitively how to nurture hearts—and their commitment to doing so was held with warrior-like fierceness.

If the image of a warrior seems incongruent to you when thinking about a positive workplace where everyone is flourishing, expand your understanding to include the total picture of a truly effective warrior. A warrior is much more than someone who learns to gain power over others through combat or warfare. The intense energy of a warrior can be channeled for peaceful purposes to gain influence *with* others.

A warrior's true essence is about being fearless in pursuit of goals—about courage, relentlessness, and achievement. Peace, perseverance, and hard work—the peaceful warrior's way—are the ways to reach one's goals. The spiritual warrior is on a quest for self-knowledge and the ability to serve others with this knowledge. As the leader who brings the Positivity Pulse to your workplace, you are stepping onto the path of the spiritual warrior.

KEYS TO SUCCESS

Creative Recognition is one more tool that enables you to cultivate employees' willingness, interests, and creativity by creating moments where success is inescapable—and then you give the employee all of the credit for that success.

Positivity Pulse Points

- Your values serve your employees and your customers and create a culture of shared beliefs that lead to your rules. Compliance can then be understood as a way to support the organization's values.

- Precisely state the workplace rules and policies in the negative. State "No…" so that everyone understands exactly where the boundary lies.

- Liberally give Proactive Recognitions during the day by noticing and recognizing employees when they are *not* breaking rules. In doing this, employees come to feel seen and appreciated for being great employees that are upholding the rules, policies, and most importantly, the values of your organization.

- When not making requests, be as creative as possible in seeing opportunities to energize employees for their choices. Energize each increment the employee moves in the right direction of success.

- If you have particularly challenging employees who are resistant to the flow of positive energy, offering Creative Recognitions frequently throughout the workday or work shift can create a flow of success and positivity, breaking down resistance and opening hearts to a new and better way of relating. Don't give up! This may be the first time that employee has been kindly treated or noticed in positive ways.

- Be fearless and relentless in the pursuit of your goals to create a positive workplace where everyone flourishes!

ACTION STEP 1: Choose one rule that seems to be broken during the workday. For example: "No personal cell phone use during work." Use Proactive Recognitions to notice and verbally acknowledge when employees are not breaking the rule. List the rule you will work with this week:

_____

_____

ACTION STEP 2: Show your co-workers you are not holding yourself to a different standard. Find at least one time EACH day this week when you can reset yourself out loud and in front of at least one other person. As you gain confidence in doing this, challenge yourself to a personal reset in front of several people, perhaps in a meeting. Notice the reactions you experience. List some things for which you can reset yourself:

_____

_____

ACTION STEP 3: Choose one or two employees who need to be drawn in a more successful direction. Energize them as often as possible with Creative Recognitions whenever you catch them about to break a rule they have trouble complying with so they get disrupted before they do it. Then energize them afterward and name the difficulty they are having and give them heaps of recognition for complying. For example, "Jeremy, I see you are about to go outside to smoke and I need you to go all the way out to the smoking area." Then after he does, say, "I realize you would have liked to stop just outside the door, but you demonstrated strength of character by respecting your fellow co-workers and going all the way out to the smoking area. Thank you so much for being so considerate." List the employees and what you might say to them:

_____

_____

(NOTE: Be purposeful to honor those whom are in compliance around the rule breaker. The rule breaker then begins to download new software that rule compliance is what is energized.)

Answer the following questions:

1. What did you set out to do by starting this module?

_____

_____

_____

2. What did you accomplish?

_____

_____

_____

3. What do you need to change to be the person you want to be?

_____

_____

_____

4. What is the Pearl of Positivity Wisdom you received this week?

_____

_____

_____

5. What is your Action Step **WOWEE** (Within One Week to Energize and Excel) intention you will commit to for this upcoming week?

_____

_____

_____

ASSESSMENT MODULE #

6

"Imagine a workplace where every individual at every level is shining in goldenness and positivity, flourishing with creative ideas and brilliance that steadily increase their productivity. The workplace comes to shine because each individual is shining."

~ Sherry Blair

NOTES

IGNITE

MODULE 7

Flourish!
Ignite Your Greatness

What a long way you have come over the last several weeks as you have been working to shift the energy of your workplace to radiate pulsing positivity! In working the steps, you have also personally grown and transformed as you have discovered how to step more fully into your own greatness.

Cultivating positivity in your organization has another important benefit: it promotes peace and an environment that allows for optimal functioning. In this module we'll take a look at the connection between these two things. You will also learn how to expand positivity into the wider reaches of your organization, and a few more Action Steps to ignite flourishing in your workplace on a daily basis.

Following the steps in this module will enable you to ignite your greatness and grow your positivity so you and your workplace will continue to blossom and flourish.

Module 7 Objectives

- To review the steps you have learned.

- To realize that the power to be the change you want to see lies *within* you.

- To realize you can work proactively to create peace and harmony, both for yourself and your team.

- To empower you to be relentless and fearless with integrating your new style of communication at work, home, and play.

MODULE 7

Module 7 Summary

- Recognizing and receiving acknowledgement for your own greatness allows you to open to the gift of receiving from others.

- Review key learning from previous modules.

- Greatness practice increases flourishing.

- Cultivate peace to enable optimal experiences.

Be Willing to Receive Acknowledgement for Your Own Greatness

As odd as it may sound to you now, many of us resist being recognized for what we do right. Being recognized for the greatness inherent in our everyday actions can be a much bigger stretch. The same goes for adopting an approach to interacting with others that is consciously positive.

Upbringing plays a big role in this regard. Most parenting emphasizes and energizes negativity, even so-called positive parenting, and for many of us conflict resolution and effective communication is learned in the context of problems and challenges, not as proactive ways of relating to others. Forms of communication that energize the positive are usually learned only as problem-solving tools. By the time we learn those techniques, most of us are hardwired to manage strong negative feelings through dysfunctional means of communicating. Most of us are working against a good deal of conditioning as we resolve to refuse to energize negativity.

In learning to bring a Positivity Pulse to your workplace you have "downloaded new software" to make this change. Opening to receive the gift of being seen and acknowledged by others will help open your heart to seeing the greatness in others. You have learned techniques from this program that will enable you to practice speaking the language of nonviolence and positivity. Keep resetting yourself into this new and healing way of relating. Your major role in leadership is to be relentless and fearless with implementing this new style in your workplace. Set the example. People will get used to it whether they like it or love it.

Let's review the steps you have learned in the last few weeks:

In Module 1 you read the illustrative fable *"Creative Recognitions,"* which introduced you to characters whose characteristics might remind you of various people at work.

- **Whom did you identify with?**

- **Which character did you decide you would like to be more like?**

MODULE 7

Module 2 introduced you to recent science supporting calls for a paradigm shift towards heart-centered leadership, the Science of Happiness at Work, the broaden-and-build theory of positivity, and the Positivity Ratios.

- What things were the most impactful for you?

- Were you surprised to learn that *decreasing negativity* is a key component to *increasing* the Positivity Ratio?

Module 3 introduced you to the Four Foundational Concepts of the Nurtured Heart Approach®.

- How does the concept of "Leaders are their employees' favorite toys" hold true for you?

- How has learning to use the concept of Baby Steps helped you encourage others?

Module 4 taught you about the Three Stands™ that support the methods of the NHA, why values are important to establish before setting rules, and why it is important to state rules in the negative.

- How has becoming aware of leaking energy affected your interactions with others?

- What values have you adopted and why?

In Module 5 you discovered how to use Active Recognitions and Experiential Recognitions, as well as how to explore your character strengths and those of your team.

- In the course of the day, did using recognitions affect your own positivity?

- Were you surprised at the character strengths people guessed for you?

In Module 6 you learned and practiced advanced strategies to spiral positivity, how to relate the organization's values to the rules, and how to reset yourself back to greatness.

- In using Proactive Recognitions with employees that needed a little nudging, what was your experience?

- What was it like to practice resetting yourself?

Greatness Practice

In Glasser and Block's 2009 book *You Are Oprah: Igniting the Fires of Greatness*, the authors turned us onto what Glasser calls "greatness practice," the use of the Nurtured Heart Approach® on oneself to cultivate and expand into greatness. Greatness practice supports you in using the NHA to shine light on the greatness in yourself, colleagues, family members, lovers, partners, and spouses to build stronger, positive, and deeper relationships—in other words—to flourish! If you aren't a fan of Oprah, don't be discouraged from reading the book or using the greatness practice: Glasser uses Oprah as an example of someone who lives the example of taking herself to the greatest heights, not only for her own gain but in order to nurture greatness in others.

The more you practice this approach to create a Positivity Pulse not only in your workplace but in your life, the more you will realize the power lies within you to be the change you want to see.

You might have been raised with the understanding that greatness is awarded by the judgment of others, but greatness truly comes from within: it's a state of being. Most of us can fluently describe the greatness of others but have a difficult time accepting and appreciating our own accomplishments.

To support yourself in standing in your own greatness, complete and savor the following worksheet.

POSITIVITY
PULSE
FOR ORGANIZATIONS

Worksheet #20: *"Be the Change You Want to See"*   Date: _____

(Adapted from Glasser's "Top Eight to Being Great," as described by blogger and author Janice Taylor at The Huffington Post)

1. Accept it: your greatness is inherent, inborn, a birthright of being human. To reject this self-evident truth doesn't negate it but it negates your power to express your greatness. So begin to step into your greatness now and list some of your great qualities.

   _____

   _____

2. See it: train yourself in the art of answering this question: "What's going strong with me?" Choose to see the things you think, say, and do that are right, and the things that are going right. Choose to see the things that could be going wrong but aren't. This is an art and like all art forms it requires practice and the ability to see things anew. List some things that are going strong for you.

   _____

   _____

3. Think it: choose to dwell, to linger, to consider everything that's right that you've diligently trained your new eyes to see. For example, rather than ruminating on your impatience, you choose to dwell on the split-second of patience prior to impatience. That's using your energetic power to expand your patience to ignite your greatness. List a quality now that you are expanding into greatness.

   _____

   _____

4. Appreciate it: choose to be grateful for the greatness and the goodness that you are now able to see. What are you thankful for?

   _____

   _____

5. Feel it: emotions are so powerful that they sometimes scare us. Sometimes we try to stuff down, deny or outrun our feelings. But feelings come from our hearts and our hearts are the vehicles for transmitting greatness. Our misperception is that we have to act on every feeling. The truth is that you need only feel them. Feel them with every cell of your body and you'll be tapping into your life force. What feelings have you tried to stuff down that you will practice feeling now?

_____

_____

6. Do it: when you accept your inherent greatness and practice seeing it, thinking it, and feeling it then there's no stopping you from manifesting greatness in your actions. You are the force of unstoppable greatness at work, at home, and in your relationships. What great things have you not done because you did not believe or express your greatness that you will now do?

_____

_____

7. Be it: in consistently choosing the greatness practice it eventually becomes you. You're no longer concerned about "doing it" or "doing it right," you simply are. It is an internal state of being that aligns spirit, soul, and body. What does it feel like to be in alignment and congruent with who you really are at your core?

_____

_____

8. Live it: the final stage is self-transformation and co-creation. Your soul gets to fulfill itself and bring your greatness into the world as a manifestation of who you really are. What greatness qualities, traits, and characteristics have you longed to bring out that you can now fearlessly manifest?

_____

_____

W O R K S H E E T #

20

In a sense, as leaders, it is incumbent upon us to turn the tide of negativity in our workplaces. Moving into a peaceful harmonious working environment starts within us as individuals.

Like learning a new language, sustaining a Positivity Pulse in your workplace takes practice and perseverance. It demands that you stop leaking your own negativity while holding a mindset that is governed by open-mindedness and open-heartedness.

> **85% of the stuff study participants worried about in a two week period actually had outcomes that were positive. Also, 79% of the time worriers coped with different negative outcomes better than they expected they would. (Leahy, 2005)**

Cultivate Peace to Build Optimal Functioning

On the way to creating a Positivity Pulse in your workplace something magically happens—your workplace naturally becomes a more peaceful place to work. What do you think of when you think of peace? For some, the word peace brings to mind its opposite: war and violence. The absence of these things we might think of as peace. But peace is more than the absence of violence. It is about harmony and balance and positivity. It is something you have to create proactively—not simply through attempts to eliminate conflict.

As you have learned in this program, creating a peaceful and positive workplace requires focused intention to nurture positivity, and taking action to create a space free from hostility and inappropriate negativity through heart–centered communication, both towards yourself and others. It requires efforts to expand your connections to include new, healthy relationships. Practicing heart-centered communication can also help to heal existing relationships that have been damaged by abuse or ignorance.

In industrialized countries we have, to some degree, lost the collective tribal spirit of brotherhood and sisterhood prevalent in other countries—the spirit that understands the dynamic balance of true peace. Learning the Nurtured Heart Approach® and applying it to achieve a Positivity Pulse is extremely helpful in reintroducing that lost spirit of community and helping navigate what,

for some, may be a pretty steep learning curve into a more peaceful and positive workplace.

Cultivating peace is achieved though the willingness to see and appreciate the greatness in others as well as yourself, and using compassionate communication—the kind of communication supported by the Nurtured Heart Approach®. When you practice the strategies of NHA, you are conveying the message: you matter. The recipient receives recognition simply by virtue of being. This communication promotes peace and builds relationships that matter.

Creating a workplace rich in positive relationship naturally removes the restraint of negativity and creates a peaceful but positively energized environment that allows for a heightened level of performance. Employees are more likely to be able to enter a state of "flow," first discovered and named by Mihaly Csikszentmihalyi, a major contributor to the modern positive psychology movement. (Csikszentmihalyi 1990) In this state of optimal experience, intensity blossoms, sense of time is lost, and there is total engagement with the activity at hand.

Pause for a moment to hold this vision in your leader's heart of all your employees totally enraptured with performing their work at their highest level. Breathe. Meditate on the magnificence of your workplace.

Positivity Pulse For Organizations

143

MODULE 7

Take Action!

If you would like to spread the scope of the Positivity Pulse in your organization begin with the following steps:

1. Create a sense of urgency. In business guru John Kotter's work, the sense of exigency, as opposed to a more laissez-faire approach, is held up as the key to making real changes happen. (Kotter, 1996) If you wish to create real change in your workplace, convey a sense that the moment for change is now. Vividly imagine all employees flourishing. Remember: Investing in Human Capital by increasing Psychological and Social Capital = Improved Workplace Relations and Increased Productivity. HC(PC x SC) = IWR + $$$

2. Identify key players in your organizations who will attend the initial training. Those leaders will then function as the Nurtured Heart® warriors in your organization.

3. Schedule your initial training. Purchase reading and training materials for your entire staff. Require that your key players read these materials prior to the first training. See the resources section for information about purchasing books and hiring a Positivity Pulse trainer.

4. Dust off that policy and procedures manual. Determine what stays, what gets modified, and what goes. Be sure that you are setting clear rules and regulations including consequences for noncompliance and rule violation.

5. Host the Positivity Pulse training. Ignite the fire in your organization. Watch the transformation begin.

6. Monitor your outcomes. Keep track of ways in which the approach is helping in your organization and how its application can be continually improved.

7. Adopt a warrior stance. Maintain relentless, fearless warriorship around maintaining and increasing positivity in your organization.

8. Hold weekly meetings to receive reports on your Positivity Pulse project. Ongoing coaching and training can be done via teleconference or in person and does not need to exceed one to two hours per event.

9. Stay creative and flexible. Use your creativity to create continuous opportunities for your organization to grow into its greatness.

KEYS TO SUCCESS

- Hold to the stands.

- Apply the techniques.

- Take the Positivity Pulse Action Steps described next.

- Be creative. Come up with your own Action Steps. Watch how your workplace transforms.

Positivity Pulse Points

- Remove the energetic chaos of negative energy in the workplace and replace it with the richness of positive relationships. Positive communication allows employees to focus their intensity in a way that produces a heightened level of performance where creativity blossoms.

- Precisely state the workplace rules and policies in the negative. State "No..." so that everyone understands exactly where the boundary lies.

- Presence is what is missing from many of our relationship communications. Give the person you are interacting with your utmost attention.

- Practice kindness, humanity, empathy, service, presence, and compassionate communication.

- Real progress and lasting change require the ongoing participation of a team where everyone has an important role, knows that role, and has a stake in the outcome.

ACTION STEP 1: Identify people in your organization who will be responsible for keeping the Positivity Pulse alive. Take these action steps to keep your Positivity Pulse flourishing.

ACTION STEP 2: Let your management team and every person in your organization know that they are expected to buy into the approach. Some people may be resistant and that's okay but you may decide that your workplace may not be a good fit for them. Others may have been waiting for this kind of shift and they might surprise you with their enthusiasm!

ACTION STEP 3: Establish your organization's core values. Prioritize them. Gather feedback but know that ultimately as the leader you get to decide what those values will look like. Post them and review with your entire organization.

ACTION STEP 4: Establish a "Caring Hearts Wall of Fame" where you publicly recognize achievements, service, and any other expression of greatness in your workplace.

ACTION STEP 5: Send emails or text messages to recognize positivity as you experience it in real time. This is a great way to use technology! Don't wait. As the folks at Nike would say, just do it!

ACTION STEP 6: Reset emails and text messages that have a negative tone because they cut into productivity time. Teach the reset back to greatness. Get on the phone or meet in person to work through conflict that is being energized in a negative way via texting and emailing. Negativity energizing in emails cuts into productivity time and contributes to low morale. Some studies have shown that 80% of email messages are misinterpreted, so teach your employees to be clear in their communications.

ACTION STEP 7: Identify a person responsible for collecting and disseminating positivity news blasts via email on at least a monthly basis. Be sure this data is stored to determine eligibility criteria for Positivity Pulse awards at the end of the year. Then make it fun. Celebrate!

ACTION STEP 8: Take a stand to stop energizing negativity from this day forward.

ACTION STEPS: Module 7

ACTION STEP 9: Eliminate policies and procedures that energize negativity and modify or omit or add new ones as necessary.

ACTION STEP 10: Create clear rules, limits, and consequences.

ACTION STEP 11: Consider circulating an inspiring quote or a brief heart meditation to start the day. In only two or three minutes you can get the workforce into their hearts before the day begins.

ACTION STEP 12: Commit to energizing success in your workplace at every opportunity! Hang posters that will remind everyone in your workplace of the stands of the approach. Try using images like the Golden Gate Bridge in San Francisco or butterflies. Find images that make sense in your workplace. Think visually, auditorily, kinesthetically and experientially!

Answer the following questions:

1. What did you set out to do by starting this module?

   _____

   _____

   _____

2. What did you accomplish?

   _____

   _____

   _____

3. What do you need to change to be the person you want to be?

   _____

   _____

   _____

4. What is the Pearl of Positivity Wisdom you received this week?

   _____

   _____

   _____

5. What is your Action Step **WOWEE** (Within One Week to Energize and Excel) intention you will commit to for this upcoming week?

   _____

   _____

   _____

A S S E S S M E N T M O D U L E # 7

IGNITE

"There's no greater call than that of helping others to create lasting, deep, mutually respecting relationships and making the workplace a happier place for all. In doing so, you have an incalculable, vast, and positive influence on the lives of others. Each one you touch will touch others in turn. We salute all of you who already lead with love. And for those of you ready to take this life-changing journey, we salute you, too."

~ Alletta Bayer & Sherry Blair

NOTES

Worksheet #16: *"Practicing Active Recognitions"*   Date: _____

It feels great to be the recipient of positive recognitions. It also feels great to give them. If at first you feel awkward, GREAT! That just means you are stretching a little and learning a new way of relating. It will become easier and easier—and pretty soon it will become automatic!

Using this table to help you break down the different stages of interaction will make you aware of both sides of the interaction—the POSITIVITY PULSE.

ASSIGNMENT: At least three times in the morning and three times in the afternoon, give an Active Recognition and note it on the table below. This includes virtual recognizing in emails, texts, instant messages, instagrams, etc.

HINT: Print out pages to keep handy for use each day this week.

* Extra points for practicing and noting more than six times per day!

What You Saw or Noticed	What You Said	Recipient's Response	How You Felt

About the Authors

Alletta Bayer

As Founder of Nurtured Heart Solutions and Chief Operating Officer of The Positivity Pulse Division of Sherry Blair Institute For Inspirational Change, Alletta Bayer's mission is to empower people to unleash their highest potential in order to flourish and make a positive difference in the lives of others.

Alletta is an Advanced Trainer/Certified Nurtured Heart® Specialist and serves on the Global Summit Committee for Howard Glasser and the Nurtured Heart Approach®, a transformational approach that changes lives. She is a co-author of *The Power to Change* and *The 7 Steps to Ignite Flourishing in Leaders, Teams and Organizations* and the soon to be released *Optimize: 7 Simple Steps to Nurturing Your Heart.*

Alletta holds a Bachelor of Arts in English Literature from the University of California at Berkeley and a Master of Arts degree in Clinical Psychology from John F. Kennedy University and is a California licensed psychotherapist.

To inquire about coaching, consulting, training, and development services in your organization contact us: info@SherryBlairInstitute.com.

About the Authors

Sherry Blair

As CEO of Sherry Blair Institute For Inspirational Change, Sherry Blair inspires and motivates others by applying and encouraging Positive Psychology. She uses her skills to teach others how to build effective teams, and use non-violent communication to achieve results and resolve conflict. Teaching others to speak from their hearts is a key constituent of the work she does. Sherry is one of the first 300 in the world to be trained by Dr. Martin Seligman in his 2003 Vanguard Training, Authentic Happiness Positive Psychology Coaching Program.

Sherry graduated Rutgers University with a Bachelor of Arts in Psychology and Women's Studies. She went on to obtain her Master of Science in Social Work with a concentration in Policy Analysis and International Social Welfare at Columbia University. Dually mastered in Industrial and Organizational Psychology, supports her vision to make change at the macro level in leadership and management.

She is an Advanced Trainer/Certified Nurtured Heart® Specialist and has served on the Ethics & Global Summit Committees for Howard Glasser and the Nurtured Heart Approach®, a transformational approach that changes lives. She is also a Licensed Practitioner through The iOpener Institute in The Science of Happiness. She is the author of *The Positivity Pulse: Transforming Your Workplace* and a recent contributor to *Roadmap to Success: America's Top Intellectual Minds Map Out Successful Business Strategies with Ken Blanchard and Deepak Chopra.* She has also just released books for children and teens to ignite flourishing and leadership in the formative years, and *Optimize: 7 Simple Steps to Nurturing Your Heart* is coming soon.

To inquire about coaching, consulting, training, and development services in your organization contact us: info@SherryBlairInstitute.com.

Footnotes

Two Secrets

1. Fredrickson, Barbara *L. Positivity: Top Notch Research Reveals the 3-to-1 Ratio that Will Change Your Life.* (New York: MJF Books, 2009), 227–229.

2. Fredrickson, Barbara L. *Love 2.0: How Our Supreme Emotion Affects Everything We Feel, Think, Do, and Become.* (New York: Penguin Group, 2013), 40–41, 47–53, 54, 58, 60, 61.

3. Pryce-Jones, Jessica. *Happiness at Work: Maximizing Your Psychological Capital for Success.* (United Kingdom: Wiley-Blackwell, 2010).

Module 1

1. Jessica Pryce-Jones. "Unhappy employees only work two days a week: why happiness at work really matters." iOpener.com Press Release, August 23, 2010. Accessed February 1, 2013. http://www.iopener.com/uploads/The%20Business%20Case%20for%20Happiness%20at%20 Work%20Press%20release%20fina.pdf.

Module 2

1. Pryce-Jones, Jessica. *Happiness at Work: Maximizing Your Psychological Capital for Success.* (United Kingdom: Wiley-Blackwell, 2010).

2. Ibid, 63–148.

3. Ibid, 149–168.

4. Fredrickson, Barbara L. *Positivity: Top Notch Research Reveals the 3-to-1 Ratio that Will Change Your Life.* (New York: MJF Books, 2009), 179.

5. Jessica Pryce-Jones. "Unhappy Employees Only Work Two Days a Week: Why Happiness at Work Really Matters." iOpener.com Press Release, August 23, 2010. Accessed February 1, 2013. http://www.iopener.com/uploads/The%20Business%20Case%20for%20Happiness%20at%20 Work%20Press%20release%20fina.pdf.

6. Ibid.

7. Ibid.

8. Witt, David. "Exit Interviews Show Top 10 Reasons Why Employees Quit." Blanchard LeaderChat Forum. May 28, 2012. Accessed February 16, 2013. http://leaderchat.org/2012/05/28/ exit-interviews-show-top-10-reasons why-employees-quit/.

Footnotes

9. Ibid.

10. iOpener. "What are the Financial Benefits?" 2013. Accessed April 15, 2013. http://www.iopenerinstitute.com/what-are-the-financial-benefits.aspx?lang=en.

11. Ibid.

12. Jessica Pryce-Jones. "Can You Really Be Happy at Work?" Corp! Everything Business. June 10, 2010. Accessed March 1, 2013. http://www.corpmagazine.com/executives-entrepreneurs/executive-life/itemid/1615/can-you-really-be-happy-at-work-.

13. Pryce-Jones, *Happiness at Work: Maximizing Your Psychological Capital for Success.* (United Kingdom: Wiley-Blackwell, 2010).

14. Ibid, 149–168.

15. Fredrickson, *Positivity,* 54–119. Pg 42

16. Fredrickson, B. L., Love 2.0 The Master Class. Accessed October 29, 2013. www.MentorCoach.com.

17. Fredrickson, B. L., Positivity. Accessed October 30, 2013. www.positivityratio.com/index.php.

18. Fredrickson, *Positivity.*

19. Keyes, C. L. M. (2002). "The mental health continuum: From languishing to flourishing in life." *Journal of Health and Social Behavior,* 43(2), 207–222. doi: 10.2307/3090197

20. Fredrickson. B. L., & Losada, M. F. (2005), "Positive affect and the complex dynamics of human flourishing," *American Psychologist,* 60: 678–86.

21. Cohn, M. A., Fredrickson, B. L., Brown, S. L., Mikels, J. A., & Conway, A. M. (2009). "Happiness unpacked: Positive emotions increase life satisfaction by building resilience." *Emotion,* 9(3), 361–368. doi: 10.1037/a0015952

22. Fredrickson, B. L., Cohn, M. A., Coffey, K. A., Pek, J., & Finkel, S. M. (2008). "Open hearts build lives: Positive emotions, induced through loving-kindness meditation, build consequential personal resources." *Journal of Personality and Social Psychology,* 95, 1045-1062. doi: 10.1037/a0013262

Footnotes

23. Kok, B. E., Coffey, K. A., Cohn, M. A., Catalino, L. I., Vacharkulksemsek, T., Algoe, S. B., Brantley, M., & Fredrickson, B. L. (2013). "How positive emotions build physical health: Perceived positive social connections account for the upward spiral between positive emotions and vagal tone." *Psychological Science.* Advance online publication. doi: 10.1177/0956797612470827

24. Catalino, L. I., & Fredrickson, B. L. (2011). "A Tuesday in the life of a flourisher: The role of positive emotional reactivity in optimal mental health." *Emotion,* 11(4), 938–950. doi:10.1037/a0024889

25. Gruber, J. (2011). "A review and synthesis of positive emotion and reward disturbance in bipolar disorder." *Clinical Psychology & Psychotherapy,* 18(5), 356–365. doi: 10.1002/cpp.776

26. Fredrickson, *Positivity,* 158–178.

27. Ibid, 174–177.

28. Gottman, J. M., and N. Silver. *The Seven Principles for Making Marriage Work.* (New York: Three Rivers Press, 1999).

29. Schwartz, R. M., C. F. Reynolds, et al. (2002). "Optimal and normal affect balance in psychotherapy of major depression: evaluation of the balanced states of mind model." *Behavioral and Cognitive Psychotherapy* 30: 439–50.

30. Pryce-Jones. *Happiness at Work: Maximizing Your Psychological Capital for Success.* (United Kingdom: Wiley-Blackwell, 2010).

* Sherry Blair is an accreditee through the iOpener Institute under the United States Global Partner.

** This survey is an abbreviated version, although validated measurement derived from the comprehensive individual report. The iPPQ measures individuals, teams and entire organizations and can be utilized as a developmental tool to increase happiness at work as well as a method for tracking the progress.

Module 3

1. Glasser, Howard N., and Bowdidge, Joann and Bravo, Lisa. *Transforming the Difficult Child Workbook: An Interactive Guide to The Nurtured Heart Approach®.* (Tucson: Nurtured Heart® Publications, 2007), 24–33, 46–51.

2. McGonical, Jane. *Reality is Broken: Why Games Make Us Better and How They Can Change the World.* (New York: The Penguin Press, 2011), 354.

Footnotes

3. Blanchard, Ken and Lacinak, Thad and Thompkins, Chuck and Ballard, Jim. *Whale Done: The Power of Positive Relationships.* (New York: Free Press, 2002), Front flap.

4. Fredrickson, Barbara L. *Positivity: Top Notch Research Reveals the 3-to-1 Ratio that Will Change Your Life.* (New York: MJF Books, 2009), 74–96.

5. Welsh, Jennifer, Live Science Staff Writer. "Brains of Excessive Gamers Similar to Addicts." LiveScience.com. November 15, 2011. Accessed April 15, 2013. http://www.livescience.com/17033-gamer-brain-reward-system.html.

Module 4

1. Glasser, Howard N. with Melissa N. Block. *Notching Up The Nurtured Heart Approach®—The New Inner Wealth™ Initiative for Educators.* (Tucson: Nurtured Heart® Publications, 2007).

2. Peterson, Christopher and Martin Seligman. 2004. *Character Strengths and Virtues.* (New York: Oxford University Press, 2004).

Module 7

1. Glasser, Howard N., and Bowdidge, Joann and Bravo, Lisa. *Transforming the Difficult Child Workbook: An Interactive Guide to The Nurtured Heart Approach®.* (Tucson: Nurtured Heart® Publications, 2007), 24–33, 46–51.

2. Glasser, Howard N. with Block, Melissa Lynn. *You Are Oprah—Igniting the Fires of Greatness.* (Tucson: Nurtured Heart® Publications, 2009).

3. Janice Taylor, "You Are Oprah: Top Eight to Being Great." The Huffington Post. June 2, 2009. Accessed April 26, 2013. www.huffingtonpost.com/janice-taylor/you-are-oprah-top-eight-t-b-209633.html.

4. Leahy, Robert L. *The Worry Cure: Seven Steps to Stop Worry from Stopping You.* (New York: Three Rivers Press, 2005), 10–25.

5. Csikszentmihalyi, Mihaly. *Flow: The Psychology of Optimal Experience.* (New York: Harper and Row, 1990).

6. Kotter, John. "Leading Change." *Harvard Business Review,* 1996.

Bibliography

Blair, Sherry, Blanchard, Ken and Chopra, Deepak. *Roadmap to Success: America's Top Intellectual Minds Map Out Successful Business Strategies.* Sevierville, TN: Insight Publishing, 2013.

Blair, Sherry with Block, Melissa Lynn. *The Positivity Pulse: Transforming Your Workplace.* Seattle, WA: Createspace/An Amazon Company, 2011.

Blanchard, Ken and Hodges, Phil. *The Servant Leader: Transforming Your Heart, Heads, Hands, and Habits.* Nashville, TN: J. Countryman/Thomas Nelson, Inc., 2003.

Blanchard, Ken and Lacinak, Thad and Thompkins, Chuck and Ballard, Jim. *Whale Done: The Power of Positive Relationships.* New York: Free Press, 2002.

Catalino, L. I. & Fredrickson, B. L. (2011). "A Tuesday in the life of a flourisher: The role of positive emotional reactivity in optimal mental health." *Emotion,* 11(4), 938–950. doi: 10.1037/a0024889

Cohn, M. A., Fredrickson, B. L., Brown, S. L., Mikels, J. A., & Conway, A. M. (2009) "Happiness unpacked: Positive emotions increase life satisfaction by building resilience." *Emotion,* 9(3), 361–368. doi: 10.1037/a0015952

Csikszentmihalyi, Mihaly. *Flow: The Psychology of Optimal Experience.* New York: Harper and Row, 1990.

Davis, Orin. "Why the Workplace Needs Positive Psychology." (Working Paper). Accessed June 6, 2013. http://www.qllab.org/Research.html.

Bibliography

Fredrickson, B. L. Positivity. Accessed October 30, 2013. www.positivityratio.com/index.php.

Fredrickson, Barbara L. *Positivity: Top Notch Research Reveals the 3-to-1 Ratio that Will Change Your Life.* New York: MJF Books, 2009.

Fredrickson, Barbara L. *Love 2.0: How Our Supreme Emotion Affects Everything We Feel, Think, Do, and Become.* New York: Penguin Group, 2013.

Fredrickson, B. L. Love 2.0 The Master Class. Accessed October 29, 2013. www.MentorCoach.com.

Fredrickson, B. L., Cohn, M. A., Coffey, K. A., Pek, J., & Finkel, S. M. (2008). "Open hearts build lives: Positive emotions, induced through loving-kindness meditation, build consequential personal resources." *Journal of Personality and Social Psychology,* 95, 1045–1062. doi: 10.1037/a0013262

Fredrickson, B. L., & M. F. Losada (2005), "Positive affect and the complex dynamics of human flourishing." *American Psychologist* 60: 678–86.

Freiberg, Jackie and Freiberg, Kevin. *GUTS: Companies that Blow the Doors Off of Business-as-Usual.* New York, NY: Currency/Doubleday, 2005.

Glasser, Howard N. with Melissa N. Block. *Notching Up The Nurtured Heart Approach®—The New Inner Wealth™ Initiative for Educators.* Tucson: Nurtured Heart® Publications, 2007.

Bibliography

Glasser, Howard N. with Melissa Lynn Block. *You Are Oprah—Igniting the Fires of Greatness.* Tucson: Nurtured Heart® Publications, 2009.

Glasser, Howard N., and Joann Bowdidge, and Lisa Bravo. *Transforming the Difficult Child Workbook: An Interactive Guide to The Nurtured Heart Approach®.* Tucson: Nurtured Heart® Publications, 2007.

Glasser, Howard N., and Jennifer L. Easley. *Transforming the Difficult Child: The Nurtured Heart Approach®.* Tucson: Nurtured Heart® Publications, 1998.

Gottman, J. M., and N. Silver. *The Seven Principles for Making Marriage Work.* New York: Three Rivers Press, 1999.

Gruber, J. (2011). "A review and synthesis of positive emotion and reward disturbance in bipolar disorder." *Clinical Psychology & Psychotherapy*, 18(5), 356–365. doi: 10.1002/cpp.776

iOpener. "Unhappy Employees Only Work Two Days a Week: Why Happiness at Work Really Matters." Press Release, August 23, 2010. Accessed February 1, 2013, http://www.iopener.com/uploads/The%20Business%20Case%20for%20Happiness%20at%20Work%20Press%20release%20fina.pdf.

iOpener. "What are the Financial Benefits?" 2013. Accessed April 15, 2013, http://www.iopenerinstitute.com/what-are-the-financial-benefits.aspx?lang=en.

Bibliography

Keyes, C. L. M. (2002). "The mental health continuum: From languishing to flourishing in life." *Journal of Health and Social Behavior, 43*(2), 207–222. doi: 10.2307/3090197

Kok, B. E., Coffey, K. A., Cohn, M. A., Catalino, L. I., Vacharkulksemsek, T., Algoe, S. B., Brantley, M., & Fredrickson, B. L. (2013). "How positive emotions build physical health: Perceived positive social connections account for the upward spiral between positive emotions and vagal tone." *Psychological Science.* Advance online publication. doi: 10.1177/0956797612470827

Kotter, John. "Leading Change." *Harvard Business Review,* 1996.

Leahy, Robert L. *The Worry Cure: Seven Steps to Stop Worry from Stopping You.* New York: Three Rivers Press, 2005.

McGonical, Jane. Reality is Broken: Why Games Make Us Better and How They Can Change the World. New York: The Penguin Press, 2011.

Peterson, Christopher and Martin Seligman. 2004. *Character Strengths and Virtues.* New York: Oxford University Press, 2004.

Pryce-Jones, Jessica. "Can You Really Be Happy at Work?" Corp! Everything Business. June 10, 2010. Accessed March 1, 2013. http://www.corpmagazine.com/executives-entrepreneurs/executive-life/itemid/1615/can-you-really-be-happy-at-work-.

Bibliography

Pryce-Jones, Jessica. *Happiness at Work: Maximizing Your Psychological Capital for Success.* United Kingdom: Wiley-Blackwell, 2010.

Randolph, John. (2013). *Reward and Recognition at Work: What's the Brain Got to Do With It?* APA Center for Organizational Excellence: Good Company Vol. 7 No. 5. Accessed May 25, 2013, http://www.apaexcellence.org/resources/goodcompany/newsletter/article/447.

Schwartz, R. M., C. F. Reynolds, et al. (2002), "Optimal and normal affect balance in psychotherapy of major depression: Evaluation of the balanced states of mind model." *Behavioral and Cognitive Psychotherapy,* 30: 439–50.

Seligman, Martin E. P. *Authentic Happiness: Using the New Positive Psychology to Realize Your Potential for Lasting Fulfillment.* New York: The Free Press, 2002.

Seligman, Martin E. P. *Flourish: A Visionary New Understanding of Happiness and Well-being.* New York: Free Press, 2011.

Welsh, Jennifer, Live Science Staff Writer. "Brains of Excessive Gamers Similar to Addicts." LiveScience.com. November 15, 2011. Accessed April 15, 2013. http://www.livescience.com/17033-gamer-brain-reward-system.html.

Witt, David. "Exit Interviews Show Top 10 Reasons Why Employees Quit." Blanchard LeaderChat Forum. Last Modified May 28, 2012. Accessed February 16, 2013. http://leaderchat.org/2012/05/28/exit-interviews-show-top-10-reasons-why-employees-quit/.